The Golfer's Wife

Stay out of the rough!

Best,

Janet Thompson

amplifypublishing.com

The Golfer's Wife

©2022 Janet Thompson. All Rights Reserved. No part of this publication may be reproduced, stored in a retrieval system or transmitted in any form by any means electronic, mechanical, or photocopying, recording or otherwise without the permission of the author.

For more information, please contact:
Amplify Publishing, an imprint of Mascot Books
620 Herndon Parkway, Suite 320
Herndon, VA 20170
info@mascotbooks.com

Library of Congress Control Number: 2021917264

CPSIA Code: PRFRE0122A
ISBN-13: 978-1-63755-106-6

Printed in Canada

This book is dedicated to my husband, Steve, "The Golfer."
Without him, I would never have ventured onto a golf course.

I would also like to thank my two daughters, Laura Stoll and
Emily Johannsen. Their love, encouragement, and much-
needed computer technical support along the way in writing
this book have been invaluable to me.

The Golfer's Wife

From **Birdies** to **Quadruple Bogies** and the **Rough in Between**

JANET THOMPSON

CONTENTS

INTRODUCTION

For some, golf is an instant passion. These golfers practice religiously, play often, watch it on TV, and frequently attend tournaments.

Then there's the other kind of golfer. This group simply enjoys the occasional round and doesn't take the game too seriously.

Things get interesting when these two kinds of people marry each other.

It has been over thirty-five years since I married Steve, an extremely passionate golfer who has always approached the game with all the vigor and obsession of the pro leagues. I was a non-golfer when we married and had no idea what direction life would take after the "I dos."

I have talked to numerous wives about their relationships with their golf-loving husbands and have observed the couples playing golf together. Many of the wives are just like me: they take up the sport to spend a little more time together. Other wives are content to have their husbands disappear for five or more hours! I say, go with whatever works to make each other happy. Too many marriages these days fall apart over lots of issues; why make golf one of them? I realized a long time ago, if I truly loved the man, why would I want him to give up something that he is so ardent about? I simply chose to become "The Golfer's Wife."

A professional golfer's wife has to take on this role even further in order to have a successful marriage and family life. She becomes the cheerleader, travel agent, nutritionist, therapist, periodic single parent, world traveler, household manager, and more. This wife is juggling more things than I ever could have, and keeping the schedule straight is a whole other story!

Professional golfers are well known for their personalities and most especially by their rankings. Their spouses are thrust into the spotlight when their husbands win a tournament, and they jump from behind the rope for a quick kiss and photo. Their children, if present, join in the media circus. Most of the time their private lives are hidden from the public. A few of them even choose to hide their "spouse" badges, so you have no idea who you're standing next to at a tournament. Be careful what you say!

Here, I've written the book I would have loved to have thirty-six years ago. I hope it makes a difference in other golf spouses' love/less-than-love relationship with the game, and, beyond that, entertains both the golfer and nongolfer.

With this book, I also hope to raise awareness and funds for the following charities. They are very close to the hearts of the professional golfer's wives and mine as well. I'd love nothing more than for you to check out the websites to contribute and otherwise support these charities. Proceeds from this book, too, will be donated to the charities. In this way, we can turn what we do for play into something that changes the world. Thank you for purchasing this book and supporting all of them.

See you on the links!

- The Brandt & Mandy Snedeker Foundation
- Brighter Days Foundation
- Charley Hoffman Foundation
- Crystal Coast Hospice House
- Micaela's Army Foundation
- The Jacobsen Youth Initiative
- Juvenile Diabetes Research

1 Why I Play

Every golfer has to start somewhere. I started with Steve.

For me, at twenty-seven, it was a blind date that finally went right. The dating game is always challenging and exhausting when you're looking for "the one," but even so, I still got a surprise ending.

During a party at their home in the Chicago suburbs, my sister and her husband set me up with their friend Steve. Three of my sisters and my two brothers were also there. It was efficient, anyway. Why not just meet the whole family and get that part out of the way?

The evening went well, so Steve and I headed to a local pizza place and sports bar called Marnie's. We talked about many things; golf might have been mentioned. But if it was, I wouldn't have really noticed. The only thing I knew about golf was from my brother John, who was a caddie at the country club nearby.

John worked as a caddie every weekend at the Hinsdale Golf Club, both Saturday and Sunday. That should have been my first clue as to how much time the sport involves, but hey, loads of people had weekend jobs. He also came home with boatloads of cash and some hilarious stories. It made me wonder sometimes, *What kind of person belongs to these exclusive clubs anyway?*

Somehow, Steve and I went on to have a whirlwind courtship even without full disclosure of his second love (at least, I think it's his second). I don't recall him playing that much golf through all that. Love sure is blind, isn't it? We were engaged in six months and married on April 20, 1985. The honeymoon was great—two heavenly weeks in gorgeous Cancun, Mexico.

We explored white, sandy beaches, the ruins in Tulum, the Isle of Mujeres, and all of the great restaurants. That was week one. The second week, Steve casually proposed playing a round of golf at Pok Ta Pok. That would be a nice change of pace, right? You could rent clubs right there, he told me, and I could ride in the golf cart.

Little did I know I was getting my first sample of Steve in his true element. Did I mention we were married already? That day, he made golf look effortless, and I enjoyed the beautiful weather and scenery. Still, I had no idea how important golf was to him.

We embarked on our life together. During that first year, I may have picked up a club or two. Steve—hint, hint—even made me my own set! He bought the parts and put them together himself. Ha ha, very customized for the novice golfer, me! He would regrip them as a hobby and save some money, too. We had two Bibles in our house: the real one and Ralph Maltby's *Golf Club Design, Fitting, Alteration and Repair*. Imagine the angst when our Maltby's was lost on our second move, from Carmel, Indiana, to Orland Park, Illinois. I took pity on Steve that Christmas and purchased the newest edition; several years later, we discovered the original in a box we forgot to unpack.

Once I caught onto how much Steve was into the game, I tried my best to learn. However, I am probably not the first to conclude that my relationship with golf would always be a love/hate one. You love it when the little white ball goes where you want it to, but you hate it when it does not. There seems to be nothing in between.

Two weeks before our first anniversary, I discovered I was pregnant. In the thrill of expecting a baby, the minimal skills that I had acquired on the green went right down the drain. The golf swing is already not a natural movement, by any stretch of the imagination. If someone tells you otherwise, they are either drunk or just plain ignorant. Contorting and turning the body with the perfect form and tempo to achieve an effective swing is hard enough; doing it with a basketball-sized bundle at your midsection presents an insurmountable challenge. For me, it was an easy out. My pregnancy allowed me to enjoy the spa life when we traveled instead of torturing myself on the links. I joked with Steve that it would only be fair if I got to spend as much money at the spa as he did on the course.

Our basketball bundle of joy, Laura, arrived in November 1986. Six months later, I was pregnant with baby girl number two, and Emily was born in February 1988. Having two little ones fifteen months apart was a full-time job for me that didn't allow for leisurely days on the golf course—another easy out. My clubs were put in a closet, not to see the light of day for a long time.

I thoroughly enjoyed being home with the girls. I didn't miss golf at all. New family man Steve, on the other hand, had to whittle it down to one day each weekend—the other day was mandated to family time. He sometimes still went into withdrawal, so he would watch golf on TV while playing with the girls in the family room. It worked as long as the girls were entertained and stayed within the ten-foot space in front of the screen.

In May 1989, Steve took a new job in Indianapolis, Indiana, for an industrial construction company. While he interviewed, I scoped out the neighborhoods. I found the perfect home, and he was offered the position. I have no doubt that his having played golf with them when he was a contractor was a big factor.

I was philosophical about his time on the course while we were in Indianapolis. Steve got in an extra round of golf each week, and it made for a happier husband and father. It amazes me how much business is conducted on the golf course. One of Steve's good friends plays in tournaments all over the country, and the company he works for does not count that as time off. I call that monkey business! What a perfect set up: you get paid to play and have fun.

We moved into a stunning home in Carmel, Indiana. It was even decorated to our tastes, so we did not have to do a thing. The new house was located in a wonderful neighborhood with tree-lined streets and lots of children. I soon found out that Pam, my neighbor across the street, played golf. She came complete with twin eleven-year-old daughters who liked to babysit. I was used to an older babysitter, but $11 + 11 = 22$, so I went with it (as long as Pam was home). This was in the late 1980s.

Pam belonged to a nine-hole league and asked me to join. Maybe it was time to break out those clubs again. A nearby church had a mom's-day-out program, so I signed up and joined the league. The church program gave me four hours to myself in which to socialize and play golf. I was nervous about leaving the girls, but after a few tears, they were both happy playing with other children. As for me, I found myself wondering if I could still hit that little white ball with any consistency.

The first time I was out on the links again, I played with Pam, but after that the league captain made the pairings. My game was rusty, and it made me anxious to play with people I didn't know. Again, the golf swing is not a natural movement. Every Tuesday, I would pray that I would play with women who were not so good—or that it would rain. If it rained, I would drop the girls off and have a shopping day and lunch with Pam.

On one particular day, the skies were clear, and I got paired up with some really great players. Off I went, with a knot in my stomach and my knees shaking. Calming down some by the third hole, I looked at the flag and aimed for it. It was a great shot—but that wasn't the hole we were on! I didn't know the course that well, and not one person in the group spoke up and said anything.

It took a lot of self-control not to shout out some foul words. But I guess all's fair in love and golf. After finishing the round, I thought to myself, *Are you crazy? You only get four precious hours off once a week, and you are torturing yourself on the golf course!* That was my last day playing golf in Carmel. My sanity returned shortly thereafter.

Time flew by in Indiana, and Steve was transferred back to the Chicago area two years later, at the end of 1990. Our new home was in the Southwest suburbs, where painted on the water tower is "Orland Park: World's Golf Center." Sometimes you just can't fight it. Once again, I picked up those sticks. Our home was located within a half mile of a tiny golf course called White Mountain. It has a driving range and is predominately a par-3 course. We were also four miles from a private country club called Crystal Tree. By then, even the girls had plastic golf clubs for the backyard. We were clearly surrounded by golf.

Steve came home from work one day and said he wanted to take a vacation, just the two of us, to Jamaica. I thought, *How romantic and thoughtful!* Then he began telling me the details about the resort—the Tryall Club, where the Johnnie Walker World Golf Championship took place that year (1995). Oh, no. But wait! He said, "They do have a fabulous spa."

I said, "Okay, fine, let's go." The girls stayed with Steve's parents, and off we headed for romance and sunshine.

We arrived at the beautiful resort and checked in at the front desk. I anxiously asked for a brochure on the spa, and to my major disappointment, they replied, "We don't have a spa here!" I turned to my loving husband and gave him that look. Steve apologized profusely. Sometimes people hear what they want to hear. He had been sure there was a spa.

Then we got upstairs to our "suite." We opened the door, and to my shock, it contained two twin beds. I said, "This is your idea of a romantic getaway?"

Steve quickly headed back to the front desk to get us a new room, and he paid dearly for an upgrade. Thankfully, the new room was much better and had an amazing view of Montego Bay. The resort was all inclusive, so we headed to the bar and came up with a few plans. Yes, golf figured prominently!

I did find out they had a masseuse on duty, so I scheduled a Swedish massage for that evening. I really looked forward to it—massage is a treat that I don't often have. Unfortunately, Steve stayed in the room and talked with the masseuse the entire time about all the pro golfers she had met. Not the relaxing experience I had hoped for! I should have jumped off the table and gone out for a drink.

The next morning, we headed for the golf course. On this particular course, a caddie was required. Terrific! Finding the balls in the rough was always a big challenge for me. Steve truly wanted me to have fun, especially since the massage hadn't gone so well.

He instructed the caddie to kick out any ball of mine that landed in the rough and put it in the fairway. He even went so far as to instruct him to tee them up for me. Golf, as I had always been told, is a game of integrity. However, at this stage in my game, I had to break a few rules in order to make the game palatable. Believe me, I needed to take full advantage of this. Steve understood.

We finished the round and headed off to the beach. A few piña coladas later, I was feeling no pain. That evening at dinner, we met another vacationing couple, Cheryl and Bill. They also played golf, so I got hooked into another round the very next day. No more cheating for me. It would be way too embarrassing to play the way I had the day before. I told myself to suck it up and count each and every stroke.

Steve and I quickly discovered that Cheryl was the golfer of their family. She was amazingly good, and her husband Bill was average. I was clearly the worst. I would not have felt so bad if Bill had been the better player, but it is really hard on the ego to play with another woman who is so good. I got through all eighteen holes, but it was a long round, and I looked forward to drowning my sorrows on the "nineteenth hole." (In case you do not know what this is, it's the bar!)

On that vacation, if it had been up to them, my Steve and the other wife, Cheryl, would have played a round of golf every day. Her husband, Bill, and I were perfectly content to hang out on the beach. However, splitting up couples is not a good way to spend a romantic vacation, especially when it involves switching husbands. The compromise was that the next day, Steve and Bill would play golf early, and I would take Cheryl out on a sailboat. The boys joined us later on the beach. It was a great day because the water was turquoise blue, and soft tropical winds were blowing, not to mention the fact that I didn't have to play golf. Cheryl contented herself with playing the next day, again with her husband.

We had a wonderful vacation, and it was fun meeting Cheryl and Bill. But sometimes I wonder how different life would have been for Steve if he had married a great golfer like Cheryl. I think that is why I don't just throw in the towel and give up the game entirely. I feel compelled to keep trying and improving, to let him know I understand how important it is to him. I also know that I wouldn't see him as much (or at all!) if he played all the golf he wanted, and I never joined him. I do love the guy.

Every year I pride myself on beating Steve at least once on a golf hole straight up. We'll be playing eighteen holes together, and he'll miss a putt. That's my moment, and I seize it. If I don't get nervous or let him psych me out, I can beat him on that one hole. I call that a win! Even that little victory is great for the ego. That's why golfers, even bad ones, just keep coming back for more.

CINDER-ELLIE: ELLIE DAY

Jason Day certainly knows to keep his head in the game in order to handle the mental pressure of becoming the number one player in the world. Long drives, precise iron play, great chips, and clutch putts lead the way to victories. But what is it like being married to the "Number One Golfer in the World"? In September 2015, Ellie Day, one of the few people who has the personal experience to answer that question, began living that dream with her husband, Jason Day.

Married to Jason since 2009, Ellie has seen her husband's career build from early tournaments to earning that number one world ranking. But she says, "It's a lot like being married to the one hundred and seventy-fifth or the one hundred fortieth [Jason's rankings in years past]. I feel like I have to share him with the whole world, and that can be hard. I try to remind myself that this is a season of our life. We never know how long this will last. I want to be filled with gratitude for the busyness of this time. We now have a platform to raise awareness and funds for the charities that need our help."

Ellie Harvey grew up a country girl in the small town of Lucas, Ohio (between Columbus and Cleveland). As she says, "It's out in the middle of nowhere!" The thirty-five people in her high school graduating class were mostly the same ones she started out with in kindergarten.

Ellie says that she loved everything about growing up in such a small, tight-knit community. She played volleyball and softball, but her favorite activity was the Future Farmers of America (FFA). "I competed in a lot of competitions with the FFA and feel it was one of the best things that I did growing up. It taught me integrity, and I learned so much," Ellie states with pride.

The year Ellie graduated high school, a series of events happened that would change her plans for college and life drastically. Right after graduation, she was in a terrible car accident, then a friend of hers since kindergarten died of a drug overdose, and then a month later her single mother unexpectedly got remarried. On top of that, another friend died, her childhood dog died, and even her boyfriend changed his mind about going to the same college that she had planned to attend. With all of this happening so close together, Ellie was overwhelmed. She stayed home for a year instead of going to college and worked.

The time off from school helped her focus on a new pursuit, which was to cut and style hair. She moved up toward Cleveland to attend the Paul Mitchell Beauty School Academy at age nineteen. To cover her expenses, in 2005 she started working at Mavis Winkles Irish Pub after her classes. And that's when fate stepped in.

John Hoover, who had started a golf academy twenty minutes from Cleveland, was a regular at Mavis Winkles. Another regular was Colin Swatton, who was an expert caddie. They lived on Mavis's chicken wings at the bar almost every night.

Colin made the fateful introduction when Jason was in town for the golf academy. He introduced him to Ellie by saying that Jason was "this guy from Australia who played golf." Ellie thought Jason was cute but brushed off the introduction. She did not even know his last name. She had enough to think about—the job was fast-paced and hectic, especially when the restaurant was busy. Jason and Colin would sit at the bar where they could observe Ellie through a small window running herself ragged. They called her Cinder-Ellie because at the end of the night she would be scrubbing the floors. She laughed and said she really looked the part because of the apron and her messy hairdo.

About a year later, Jason randomly sent her a text message. It said, "Hey, this is Jason from Australia. Do you remember me?" Ellie thought, *This is really weird—why is he texting?* But of course, she answered. Jason texted her that entire year. He would tell her where he was playing, and they continued to chat back and forth.

By then Ellie had completed beauty school and was still working at the restaurant. Destiny struck again two years later, in June 2007, when she and Jason saw each other in person at a mutual friend's graduation party. They bonded over not being allowed to drink, since both of them were underage.

Jason invited her to attend a tournament in Cleveland that weekend for the Legend Financial Group Nationwide. It was exciting that he won; however, Ellie had no idea of the importance of that day. By winning this tournament, Jason obtained his tour card and was then eligible to compete on the PGA tour. It was the first time Ellie had ever attended a golf tournament. She nonchalantly congratulated Jason by saying, "Good job—that's great. See you later."

Their first date was that weekend. It was a little strange, since Colin decided to tag along. They went to Applebee's for dinner, and Colin asked for a cozy table for three in the corner. Ellie was sure the hostess was thinking, *What is going on?* The boys sat opposite from her, almost like an interview. She remembers they laughed a lot. After dinner, Jason told Colin that they were going to a movie. To be polite, Jason asked Colin if he wanted to join them. Jason began to panic when Colin seemed to be considering it. Lucky for them, Colin was just teasing. The movie, *1408*, was a horror film based on Stephen King's short story with the same name. Jason later admitted that taking Ellie to this scary film was a ploy to be able to hold her hand. Ellie felt terrorized and clung to him, so Jason's mission was accomplished.

The successful first date led to a long-distance relationship. Jason would fly to see her almost every other weekend, and frequent phone calls helped. The turning point came when her lease was ending in January 2008. Ellie didn't have anything really holding her to Cleveland, so Jason asked her to move to Orlando with him. But moving to Orlando was a big deal. She told him, "I don't think so. Just go back home and be with your friends, and think about what you just asked me."

Once back in Australia, Jason could not take his mind off her. He cut his trip short and convinced her to join him at his next tournament—in Hawaii. She said with a grin, "You twisted my arm." After the tournament, she would make her decision. He missed the cut, but that gave them some needed time together.

When Jason was leaving for his next tournament, Ellie said goodbye at the airport with tears in her eyes. She knew in her heart that being away from Jason any longer was not an option. The big decision was made, and she would be moving to Orlando.

She gave her two weeks' notice to Mavis Winkles. Telling her parents was a lot tougher. She waited to tell her conservative dad because she knew he would not approve. As anticipated, he tried hard to convince her not to go. But Ellie was twenty-one and had her mind made up; nothing he could say would change it. It was a difficult time.

Even though they didn't entirely approve, Ellie's parents never once said anything negative. If Ellie wanted to come home for a visit, she felt welcomed. Ellie realized that her dad would not have been a good father if he simply said, "See you later." When the marriage proposal finally came, her father was a lot happier—and so was she.

Jason brought her back to her hometown to deliver a romantic proposal on her twenty-third birthday at Mount Jeez, the highest point in the county overlooking the famous Malabar Farm, former home of Pulitzer Prize-winning author Louis Bromfield and where Lauren Bacall and Humphrey Bogart got married. Ellie says, "The scenery is breathtaking, and you can see for miles."

At Mount Jeez, Jason presented Ellie with a scrapbook filled with pictures of all of the times they had spent together the last few years. When she turned to the final page, she saw a bride and groom. On the page it read, "Will the country girl marry the city boy?" Without missing a step, Jason got down on one knee and proposed.

Ellie and Jason were married on October 3, 2009, in Bellville, Ohio. They now live exactly one hour from where Ellie grew up. Ellie and their children can be close to her parents, if they are not traveling with Jason. Their house sits high upon a hill, on a beautiful piece of property. "It's a sweet little refuge," Ellie says with a smile.

Ellie always thought she would have children at a young age, which was typical of growing up in a small country town. After some necessary surgery, she became pregnant in October 2011 with their first child. The pregnancy was not easy; she not only experienced morning sickness, but depression too. At 10:15 p.m., on July 10, 2012, she delivered a baby boy, Dash James Day.

Jason turned down playing in the British Open that year to spend some time with his newborn son and wife. Some people were not happy with this decision, but others totally understood. It was a rough transition for all of them—Dash was a challenging infant, and it was especially hard on Ellie because she experienced severe postpartum depression. Thankfully, with the support of family, friends, and her strong faith, she recovered.

It took her a long time to even think about wanting another baby.

Then in December 2014, Ellie started to mull it over. She prayed and received her answer at the end of January. Lucy Adenil Day joined the family on November 11, 2015. Arriving just in time for Jason's birthday, Lucy was an extra-special present for him. The birth's timing was also perfect because it was the off season. The family was thrilled to have a full six weeks off the road to adjust and bond with adorable Lucy. In November 2018, they became a party of five with the arrival of a third child, baby boy Arrow, named after a Psalm verse that Ellie was passionate about: "Like arrows in the hands of a warrior are children born in one's youth. Blessed is the man whose quiver is full of them" (Psalm 127:4–5). The quiver had room for one more when their fourth baby, Oz, arrived in June of 2021. On this new addition to the family, Ellie said, "He's a sweet little dream, but adjusting to four kids is wild!"

When golf season starts, Ellie really does not see Jason. She says that jokingly, but it is the truth. The general public has no idea how much time he puts into perfecting his game. Sometimes it can be frustrating. Along with the accolades of being number one came the pressure from sponsors and fans if he did not play every week. If he wasn't playing, his time could be spent with sponsorship duties, dinners, photo shoots, and intense media obligations.

Sometimes Ellie longs for simplicity. She says, "I know this is where I am supposed to be right now. Maybe sometime in the future, I would like a little tiny farm out in the country because all of my family is there right now."

Ellie would have liked Dash, Lucy, Arrow, and Oz to grow up with the simple life. "Don't get me wrong," she says. "We have a really great life. But a part of me wishes they could experience the childhood that I had, so sweet, innocent, and in a small town."

A few years ago, she went back to her hometown to do some

charity work. She brought Blessings in a Backpack, a national program, to her former grade school, Lucas Elementary in Lucas, Ohio. Blessings in a Backpack mobilizes communities, individuals, and resources to provide food on the weekends for elementary school children across America who might otherwise go hungry. It was amazing for Ellie to find that her second-, fourth-, and fifth-grade teachers were all still there at the same school. "I wish my kids had that with the same kind of programs," she says. "We were out running in the woods all the time. You could bring your pig to the fair."

Giving the children a humble upbringing is difficult with their lifestyle now. After homeschooling the children for a few years, Ellie plans to find a school for them that offers programs like the FFA, 4H, or agriculture.

Another effort that has Ellie and Jason's support is their Brighter Days Foundation, which provides funding and resources to projects and organizations with missions that match their desire to help families in need. It exists to ensure everyone has a chance for a brighter day and a brighter future.

Brighter Days has been supporting area schools since 2014, with three in Lucas and one in Westerville (Columbus area). With $60,500 in donations, the lives of children at three Ohio schools were significantly affected. The organization has provided 36,480 Ohio kids with Hunger-Free Weekends, and 20,000+ children have been fed in Hunger-Free Weekends in other cities across the nation. The end results are nourished kids who are ready to learn. With a donation of $10,000, Ellie and Jason helped pack bags for area students in King County, Washington. The Brighter Days Foundation also helped with the Memorial Tournament Volunteer Appreciation program, stuffing eight hundred bags, which helped stock up the supplies to bring relief to kids during the 2020

COVID-19 school closures.

Many different types of events bring people closer together, both happy and sad. When tragedy struck the Philippines with a typhoon on November 8, 2013, it was devastating. Jason lost his grandmother and seven other family members. For Ellie, this horrific tragedy put a face to disaster relief because of Jason's relatives. "It could have been my grandma, my aunt, my cousin, and kids who died," she says. Both Ellie and Jason wanted to help, so they partnered with Matthew 25 Ministries, a relief organization, to provide supplies for people who suffered the effects of Typhoon Haiyan. They continue this goal to make a difference with Brighter Days.

In 2015, Ellie and Jason hosted their first golf tournament to raise more funds for the foundation. The hard work is truly paying off with approximately $2 million raised over the years. The President's Cup Tournament also supports the foundation. The goal is to keep it growing so they can continue to help an even greater number of organizations. Every year they hope to raise even more funds for the charities that need it the most.

Ellie says, "All I want people to know is my heart. I am still the exact same person I have always been. In my happiest place, I am in cowboy boots and line dancing with my friends, or sitting under the stars on a big hill in the country, or snuggling my babies in my bed. Nowadays my world is so different, and at times it breaks my heart that my kids won't get that kind of simplicity that I was lucky enough to grow up with. But I strongly believe I have been put in this position for a reason. I pray that I fulfill the plan God has for my life here."

2 Golf: Relaxing or Stressful? You Decide!

I knew it would happen one of these years—we'd have to bite the bullet and join the local golf club. After all, we were living in a town called "The World's Golf Center." Was this God's plan or Steve's plan?

It had always been Steve's dream to join a club. Once we moved to Orland Park, Illinois, he talked—and talked—about how fun it would be to become members at the nearby Crystal Tree Country Club. He had played a round of golf there once and loved it. I knew it could be a big expense—club memberships are partial ownerships that include a major payment upfront along with annual dues of $1,000 to $5,000 per year, plus both monthly and maintenance fees—but who was I to squelch his dreams?

The years went by, and I finally gave in. There would be some fun perks, right? The three-member selection committee at Crystal Tree scheduled an interview to meet us in March 1999. We used the name of one of our daughter's friend's parents as our sponsor, which was the best we could come up with. We didn't think we knew any movers and shakers in our new town, even after having lived there for almost eight years.

The date arrived, and we dressed the part. I had joked to Steve that I was going to wear torn jeans and talk like I was illiterate — maybe even blacken out a tooth for good measure! But no, we put on our best country club clothes. The meeting was short and sweet. I think they wanted Steve to be a part of their club, since he was such a good golfer — and our money wouldn't hurt, either. As for me, I was just part of the package. They called us the next day to let us know that we were now part of their "exclusive" club.

We suddenly had a monthly minimum to spend at the restaurant (which simply means you might as well eat there because they will charge you, even if you haven't consumed a morsel). For our first dinner there, we all dressed up, including the girls. We had to make sure that they looked appropriate as well — not as easy as it sounds. The club had a strict "no jeans" rule. At the time, it was very challenging to dress preteen girls in anything else. Our girls literally lived in jeans.

Despite the wardrobe angst, we showed up at our reservation on time and even used the valet service. *How fancy is this?* I thought. As the hostess sat us at our table I spotted our longtime neighbors, the Butlers. *What are they doing here? Do they actually belong?*

I went over to say hello and soon found out that they were actually charter members, which means they were pioneers of the club. I went back to my table, still in shock, to relay the news. I never would have guessed they were such high rollers — they had always been so down to earth. Maybe this club could start to feel like home after all. It occurred to me that maybe they didn't talk about it because it could have seemed like they were bragging. Maybe we would know others there, too. When Steve and I received a directory, we found that there were quite a few names we recognized, although we did not yet know them well.

The very next day, I phoned Jill Butler and asked her if she was in one of the golf leagues. She told me that she was thinking about it but was still very skeptical. I said I wanted to join the nine-hole league (rather than the eighteen-hole) because those women probably wouldn't be so intimidating. Jill and I agreed we would join together, reserving the right to quit if we didn't like it.

On Tuesday, our nine-hole league started with great weather and nervous beginners—us. The opening day was a scramble—a great way to start because there is no pressure for a player to keep an individual score. In a scramble, after everyone tees off, everyone hits the next ball from the best shot. Then, depending on the format, you continue to play from the best shots until the hole is complete. No one, then, is staring at a bad individual score—you just have one cumulative score for the team. With any luck, your team will not be last. Our team did not win that day, but I was perfectly happy being in the middle of the pack.

The golf part of the day being over, we could now enjoy a delicious lunch and some cocktails. Jill and I met so many ladies that day that my biggest problem became remembering their names. I am not so good at that, but if I forget, I can always count on the staff. This is a big help. As members of country clubs, we love when our names are remembered, so the staff members are especially motivated to get it right. It makes us feel like celebrities.

Knowing people's names also helps the staff with the billing. Typically, you just sign for your purchases, but sometimes you don't even have to do that. It just so happened that there was another couple at Crystal Tree with our same last name. They were definitely party people and always had a big bar tab at the end of the month. Unfortunately for us, that first month their charges were put on our bill. We soon got it all straightened out—I was thankful we didn't have to take out a second mortgage.

The other fun thing about joining a club is the opportunity to shop whenever you want. Welcome to the pro shop. My motto is "If you suck on the golf course, at least you can look good!"

Women's golf clothing used to be quite dorky, but thanks to some young, high-fashion female pros, this is no longer the case. Most of the pros have their own clothing lines and accessories with a signature color. The dye lots vary just enough to ensure you have to buy the entire outfit.

Each year, I try to update my golf wardrobe with cool designer clothing and accessories. For traveling purposes, I usually buy two tops for each pair of shorts or "skort" (shorts that look like a skirt) that I own. Steve plays in lots of events throughout the year, and these earn us pro shop credits. I like to spend them, but sometimes he beats me to it!

Sometimes club rules actually seem to be designed to make you shop. Before we joined the club, we played once at a rather run-down public golf course. This course was out in the country and by no means a fancy place. It was a very hot day, so I wore mid-length shorts and a sleeveless shirt that had no collar. I didn't think anything of it until someone at their pro shop (even public courses have shops) said I could not play their course unless I changed my shirt. I was shocked. I used to think dress codes were only enforced in Catholic grade schools (like the one I attended as a girl). Your skirt had to be of a certain length, the neck had to be high, and your arms had to be covered. But Catholic school had nothing on this golf course.

I wasn't wearing a tank top or anything remotely risqué, but the rules were the rules. A collar or sleeves had to be there. We had driven about thirty-five minutes to get there, so I didn't have much choice but to buy a shirt from them—convenient for their bottom line! I quickly settled on a short-sleeve shirt in an interesting shade of green that I knew I would never wear again.

A good friend of mine at a country club got reported for having shorts that were too short. Just like my experience, she was forced into purchasing a new pair if she wanted to play golf that day. When she told me the story, I told her not to feel bad. The woman who made the big stink about her shorts was probably just jealous of her good-looking legs.

When we joined Crystal Tree Country Club so long ago, I did not have any expectations—I just hoped my golf game would improve. Thankfully, over the years, it did. My wardrobe also expanded with shoes that had spikes and visors with golf logos. All of my golf shirts had matching skorts or shorts, many with "fashion" prints that I have since discarded. (What was I thinking? Blame it on the '90s.) I also lost a small fortune in golf balls—dozens upon dozens have wound up in the treacherous woods and in the enormous ponds. I like to think of them resting in peace, covered in muck.

What I like about clubs is that when you join, there is an instant connection with other members. The separate leagues for nine holes and eighteen holes make it that much more intimate. You get to know people quite well when you golf with them weekly and usually have lunch together. Sometimes after a trying and frustrating round, drinks can help ease the pain. The absolute best part of a club is making new friends—many of whom will continue to be friends for life.

To my surprise, the nine-hole league I joined with Jill turned out to be fun. It made me a full-fledged club participant in my own right. Fourteen years later, I'm still swinging away and enjoying the company of some fascinating women.

My first year in the league, I often got nervous and prayed for rain every Tuesday. I was a fair-weather golfer. If it rained or was too cold, I took full advantage of there being no obligation to play. Truth be told, my favorite part is lunching with the girls afterward—my reward for having spent two-plus hours trying to hit that little white ball. Not everyone opts for white, of course. Some of the women like to use brightly colored balls, thinking they will find them easier when they go in the rough or that they bring them luck. As for me, I like using colored tees. Red ones are especially lucky for me. Golf, as you can see, is sometimes more mental than it is physical. Whatever it takes, I will do.

Another thing golf has taught me is how to conserve energy. Not that it's a lot of exercise—I always take a cart. It's the mental stress that wears on me. So, to make it even more enjoyable when I'm playing particularly badly, I will indulge in a beer or cocktail right on the fairway. Thank goodness for Elaina and Shannon, the beer-cart girls. They supply all the libations a golfer could want to help get through the round. Now at nine thirty in the morning, instead of thinking of my strategy for the course, I'm thinking, *Screwdriver or Bloody Mary?* This can make for a long round— and a lot of laughs. On occasion, there's the possibility it might relax you enough to play better. But don't count on it, especially if you're playing for high stakes.

Since I started in the league, I have made so many great friends. Many of them, apparently, share my feelings about the game. Marge impressed us by showing up with some very fancy equipment. I thought, *She must be good*—but that was so far from the truth. She didn't know how to swing a club at all. She confided in me that her husband had bought her the clubs, and she had never picked them up until that day. That was one long golf round. I think we finally ate lunch at two.

Slow play—when a round of golf takes longer than the allotted time—is a no-no on the golf course. You never want to get a nasty letter from the head pro. It is like getting a very bad report card—embarrassing, insulting, and very much your own fault. Lucky for me, I have never received one of these. Unfortunately, my husband can't say the same. When he got one, he claimed that one of the friends he was playing with was talking up a storm and playing badly. If I'm playing with a beginner golfer and notice we are backing up the course, I try to let other groups go ahead and play through. This can add lots of time to your round, but that is golf etiquette. Be polite, be ready to hit when it's your turn, and don't stand over the ball forever—those are just a few of the things my husband has drummed into my head over the years. Too bad his pal hadn't been listening in!

Overthinking usually gets most golfers in trouble. If you find yourself doing this, step away before you mess up your shot. Readdress the ball and hit with a purpose. When you address the ball, perform your tried-and-true mechanical routine—that series of exact setup movements that has been implanted in your brain. If you don't have a routine, get one. It truly helps to make for a faster round and a better score.

In a nine-hole league, generally most of the golfers are beginners or average. They want to improve their scores as well as their skills, but they also like the social aspect of the game. And if you all agree on it in advance, the rules can be a little bit . . . bendy.

One of my favorite "bends" at Crystal Tree, only for the nine-hole league, is the "one ball in the pond" rule. This applies only to the first hole, and you do have to take a one-stroke penalty before being allowed to place the ball on the other side of the pond. For a beginning golfer, this hole is never a favorite because you have to hit over a body of water to get to the pin. If you wanted to avoid the water, you would instead have to route through a small forest of trees, avoid a hazard area, skip down the narrow cart path (about two hundred feet), and then hope the ball lands safely on the other side with a lie that is playable. (The "lie" is where the golf ball comes to rest after being hit.)

On hole #1, I try to remember to tee off with a water ball—an older ball that may have a few nicks in it already. Some people switch balls when they get to the pond. This is a no-no when you are playing in a championship or general golf, but this is the nine-hole league. The majority of us have no shame! I always try to play by the rules and want to attempt hitting over this body of water, but knowing my skill level, I wouldn't want to lose an expensive ball. Therefore, I start with a water ball and switch if I forget. Professional Golf Association, please forgive me and my fellow nine-hole rule breakers.

Our league has a fun event: The Three Worst Holes Elimination. You play your regular game but can pick the three highest scores to subtract from your total score. Oh, how I badly wish that was my true nine-hole score! Sometimes even picking the worst three can be a challenge for me, especially when I have had a particularly bad round. There are too many in the running!

Contrary to what you see in the Olympics, a ten is not a good score in golf. So that our league games aren't endless, we established ten as the maximum number of strokes for any one hole. At that point, I say, "Stop the bleeding." Time to pick up and move to the next hole.

Of course, you are not having fun when you get a ten or more.

You feel frustrated, angry, embarrassed, or some other emotion that is the opposite of happiness. Where are the beer cart girls? That's the trickiest part about golf—when you're having a bad run. You have to forget about that rotten golf hole you just played and start the new one with a clear head and happy thoughts. That's why golf is a head game. Golfers, mostly professionals, often seek the help of a golf psychologist. I have not resorted to this, nor has Steve. I don't think our health insurance would cover that one!

People develop some strange habits and quirks in self-defense. For example, some develop an attachment to a certain club. Often, it's the putter. They think they can only make a putt with their magical club; otherwise, they will not be able to make the ball go into the itty-bitty cup.

Many golfers today buy the latest technology to improve their game. This process never ends. I call it the "golf bag money pit." I know golfers who own several sets of clubs but don't want to give any away because they may go back to an old club that used to work for them. I myself am guilty of this, but only because of hole #17. It is a short par 3 but has an extremely high green elevation. It's like hitting the ball straight up into the air and hoping it doesn't smack you right in your face. For this hole alone, I have quite rationally purchased three clubs. That's over $350 just to try to make it to the green.

In my defense, my skill level has improved over time. For that hole, I went from a 5 wood, to a 7 wood, and finally to a 9 wood. I want to ask the Grounds and Greens Committee, "Please don't alter hole #17—I finally have the right club for it!" It was bad enough that they renumbered the hole to #12 after a course redesign. Even after that, when I told Steve that I did par on a certain hole, he would still know which one I was talking about.

When he tells me about his round of golf ("On hole #8, the par 4 with the dog leg left and a pond on the right..."), I have to go back and think through each and every hole starting with #1 till I get to #8. That's the difference between a real golfer and one like me.

All of this rejiggering was necessary because the club acquired land for a driving range on some adjacent property. I now had no more excuses for not being able to practice. Prior to the new range, we swung in a little cage with a net and guessed if we hit the ball well. Now we had an official driving range and a new clubhouse, too. It was a good decision for the club. Most country clubs have driving ranges, and we only had one opportunity to purchase the land. The one-time assessment per member wasn't too bad. I just had to sacrifice my vacation that year and spend it at the club practicing instead.

Another fun game our league plays is the Bowling Game, where we imitate the rules of bowling on the green. Finally, a golf game where high score wins! The Bowling Game is easy for me, but I try my best not to "win" this event. Too high a score for this particular event would mess with my overall handicap—and my self-esteem.

Let me explain a little bit about the handicap system. This system was made for golfers like me who frankly suck but want to try anyway. It is supposed to level the playing field, but the Professional Golf Association (PGA) has already established a maximum handicap—and I'm already there. Please do not ask me what it is. It's humiliating. All I can say is sometimes my nine-hole score is my husband's eighteen-hole score.

The handicap is a complicated system because each golf course that you can play on is totally different. Some are easier than others. Each course has a rating and a slope printed on their score card. I'm not sure how they figure that one out, but they do. A particular golfer also has an adjusted score, which simply means that you can only have a certain maximum number of strokes on any given hole. This is called equitable stroke control, or ESC.

All three of these values are entered into an official computer somewhere, and the PGA gives you your handicap. When I looked up the PGA and how a handicap is calculated, they say, "It's not rocket science." I disagree. I may have lost a few readers at this point. It's understandable. Even when you've played for years, it's more of a "trust them; they know what they're doing" kind of thing.

Basically, you pay the USGA to compute your handicap and then use it to adjust your score when you play. When I hit eleven strokes on any given hole, I simply pick up that blankety-blank ball and move on to the next one. Things could be worse. If I were playing in an official tournament, I would have to play until the ball was physically in the hole. That means I might have to take a twenty. No, of course, I'm not that bad. (Maybe.)

On January 2, 2013, my husband walked in the door and made a big announcement. He told me his handicap had become zero! What a dream come true for him. It was time to break open the champagne and celebrate. He is now a scratch golfer—one with a handicap of zero or lower. It makes it more challenging to win any tournaments because he gets zero strokes off of anyone, but he's still pleased.

I am the proud wife. I can take some credit for his new status after supporting his games all these years. However, now people assume that I play good golf just because I am married to the man. You win some, you lose some! It used to bother me that people actually thought this. I have mellowed over the years and realize for me, it's just a game. If I go out and put added pressure on myself to play well, it usually fails. If I relax, enjoy the fresh air, the scenery, and the company of fun players, both my blood pressure and my golf score are lower.

3 Rules Are Made to Be Broken

In contrast to the nine-hole, the eighteen-hole league is for more serious golfers. They have stamina, they are more motivated to improve, and they follow all of the USGA golf rules—or at least they are supposed to. They may not know all the rules, but who really does? There are millions of them!

I recall the time at the 2013 Masters Tournament in Augusta, Georgia, when a viewer called in to advise the officials that he believed Tiger Woods had taken an illegal drop. The officials reviewed a video and decided it was a legal drop. However, on the tape, it clearly showed where his original divot was and that his drop was approximately two yards back.

Then, when asked about it in a post-match interview, Tiger stated that he dropped the ball two yards from the original spot for a better shot to the pin. By that statement, Tiger incriminated himself; he had broken Rule #26-1a (in the rule book of that time, *USGA Rules of Golf, 2012–2015*). His admission caused him to receive a two-stroke penalty from the officials. He was lucky he didn't get kicked out of the tournament for signing an incorrect score card. But another obscure rule, #33-7, saved him from that fate.

If the officials can't make up their minds, and professionals like Tiger Woods don't know every little stinking rule, how is a person like me to ever learn this "game of integrity"? The "pocket" rule book is almost two hundred pages and has more golf scenarios and situations than I could ever dream of. It's like the old Yellow Pages phone books, filled with a tremendous amount of information.

For example, take Rule #18 in the current rule book. I'm not able to quote the exact wording because I have not gotten the USGA's permission, and that's another one of their rules. (Why go through all that red tape when I just want to make a simple point?) This particular rule is about playing the ball where it lies. If you happen to be unlucky enough to hit your ball in a tree, and you see it up in those branches, yes, you need to play it from there. Good golfers almost always try to play it where it lies. It's a matter of pride—or stupidity, as the case may be.

If you find yourself climbing up the tree and somehow you happen to dislodge the ball from the branch, and the ball falls to the ground, the rules say you have now incurred a one-stroke penalty. Good to know. To avoid that, you must go down the tree, get the ball, climb back up the tree, replace the ball in its exact location before it fell, and then try to hit the ball. Do not even think about breaking branches to make your backswing easier because if you do, that's another penalty. (They thought of everything.)

Just when you thought going to the driving range and the putting green would be sufficient, you now realize you should practice your tree-climbing skills as well. Golf is a tough game—you could easily come home scratched up and bleeding. Or perhaps you searched a little too deep in the woods and ended up with poison ivy. Not to worry, the relief medicine is a staple in our medicine cabinet. It's not for me—I'm not about to venture into the treacherous woods. But my husband will—and does.

After being in the nine-hole league a few years, I found myself losing friends to the eighteen-hole league. I don't know if I had one too many glasses of wine, but one evening I decided I would sign up to be in both leagues. I would play on Tuesday with the nine-holers, Thursday with the eighteen-holers, and maybe one day on the weekend with my husband. Maybe by playing three days a week, I would get good at the game—at least, that was my logic. Maybe it was the wine talking.

On Thursday, I showed up at my tee time of 8:30 a.m., only to find I was already assigned to play in one of the better groups, which included the women's club champ that year and two other longtime members of the league. Nervous! The round started out okay, but clearly, I was outmatched. I tried hard not to let it bother me. Then one of the players in my group said to me, "Can't you play a little faster?" I nearly lost it! Should I break down in tears or throw my club at her? Neither was a good option, so I simply said, "Sorry, I'm doing the best I can." I could have played a lot faster if the ball would have just moved a lot farther in the right direction—duh.

Around the fourteenth hole, my arm was really hurting. I thought about quitting because it was at a throbbing level, but no, I couldn't have them think I was a baby. I persevered and finished the round. I didn't stay for lunch that day; I went home to ice down my arm and call my doctor. Golf injuries are very common. It can be from something idiotic, like falling out of a golf cart or standing too close to the edge of an embankment while lining up a shot. Or it can be from toughing it out through the repetitive motions of the game—also not so smart to do. The golf swing is very mechanical. Repeating exactly the smooth tempo and graceful arch of the club will result in better swings and a lower score. But it's not easy to do it right every time. A proper warm-up reduces the chances of injury. However, if you're running late, as is usually the case with me, you just jump on that first tee and swing away, hoping for the best.

Lucky for me, I have a good friend who is an orthopedic surgeon. Dr. Henry Fuentes gave me an appointment that day and took some X-rays of my left elbow, which revealed a tear in the meniscus. Two days later, I was having surgery to repair the damage.

I'm not blaming the eighteen-hole league for that mess. It's obviously the fault of the darn golf irons, or even the woods—it certainly couldn't be my lack of skills. The clubs are what's causing me to swing more often because clearly the ball is not progressing as it should toward the flagstick and the teeny little cup. Thus, they are wearing out my body parts and causing major mental stress every freaking time the ball lands in a sand trap, a heavily wooded area, or—the very worst—a pond. You get the picture. This is when my integrity is tested. To relieve some tension, I just want to fling that club—but I can't. I'm playing golf, a game of integrity, and I was the one who made the fateful mistake of signing up for the eighteen-hole league.

I said goodbye to eighteen-hole that day and haven't looked back since. The surgery went well, and I took my place back with the nine-holers the next season.

PARTNERSHIP FOR LIFE: LISA LYE

Injuries caused by the game and other health issues often either weaken or strengthen a relationship, and the one between Lisa Lye and her golf pro husband Mark Lye is a good example of the latter. Tried and tested, it has strengthened to rock-solid over the years with a lot of hard work and mutual respect.

As a young girl, Lisa Evans always enjoyed athletics, especially softball. She started playing in grade school and continued playing in leagues while she attended the University of Central Florida, from which she graduated with a degree in journalism, advertising, and public relations.

Lisa's love of sports followed her into her career. Her first job out of college in 1992 was with Sunshine Network (now Fox Sports Sun), a regional network that broadcast local coverage of professional and collegiate sporting events in the state of Florida. When a position opened up at Orlando's Golf Channel Network in the public relations department in 1995, she landed the job.

Lisa readily joined the Golf Channel's after-work softball team, but she also figured it would be a good idea to take up golf as well. First, she took a few lessons after buying some inexpensive clubs to see if she even liked the sport. "This game is definitely a challenge, especially to learn as an adult," Lisa says. However, it did help that she played softball, which gave her an edge with good hand/eye coordination. It wasn't long before she was actually enjoying the game.

It was also at the Golf Channel that Lisa met professional golfer and PGA Tour winner Mark Lye in 1995. He was recovering from a golf-related torn ligament in his right hand and working as an analyst. Lisa would set up his interviews and help promote the Golf Channel as well. At first, she wasn't sure that Mark even knew who she was, but he surprised her one day when he asked her out. The relationship blossomed.

They had to keep the situation quiet on the work front due to a no-dating policy, but everyone else in their lives soon saw them as a couple. "It was hard!" Lisa says now. They were in love and happy but couldn't show it at work. On the other hand, as Lisa tells it, "I have to say, it made it a little exciting."

At least Mark did not work out of the office consistently. He traveled frequently and lived down in Naples. "He would come to Orlando and would be there for a while," Lisa says. "It was a little awkward." She continues with a laugh, "My boss did eventually figure it out because Mark would be so standoffish to me in the office. If my boss and I were standing there, he would direct the entire conversation to her as if I weren't there." After a while, the boss caught on. But she was a friend, too. She was okay with keeping it quiet.

Lisa had continued to take golf lessons, but after dating for a year, Mark offered to be her instructor. Lisa wondered if the notorious coach/student tension for dating couples might be the end of the relationship, but she said yes anyway. Mark turned out to be a great teacher. He even gave her brand-new clubs for her birthday.

When Lisa and Mark eventually got engaged, one of them had to leave the station. "I knew it would be easier for me to find another position," Lisa says. "Orlando as a city was growing by leaps and bounds, so it was time for me to get out of there. Mark lived in Naples, which I really liked. So, I moved down there. He wanted me to travel with him anyway."

Lisa left the Golf Channel and began doing some consulting work. "I would do PR for some of the golfers on the different tours," she says. "It was something I could do on the road. Then I started taking over trying to get deals for Mark with golf companies, and the two of us started helping them put on corporate outings and charity events. That took on a life of its own and became a whole other job. We did that for a long time." She and Mark were married on March 14, 1999. They've been in business together ever since—they really work well as a team.

Life as a golfer's wife can be glamorous. If your husband is playing well, you might take a private jet to an event or share a plane with other tour players. Lisa has done some things she never imagined she would get to do, like meet Alice Cooper and singer/guitarist Glenn Frey of the Eagles. Growing up, her dad and sister were big Eagles fans. The Monday after the Master's Golf Tournament every year, Hootie & the Blowfish have a celebrity pro-am tournament that Mark and Lisa always attend. This is a fun event for the whole family and has become one of the largest fundraisers in South Carolina.

Mark and Lisa were in the early part of their dating when he appeared in the golf movie *Happy Gilmore* in 1996. Sadly, she was not at the red-carpet ceremony. However, she was there to enjoy some hilarious lyrics of Jake Trout and the Flounders, the cover band that Mark was in with fellow professional golfers Payne Stewart and Peter Jacobsen.

The band was "basically a spoof," Lisa remembers. For the release of their second album in 1999, she says, "They set this whole party up at Planet Hollywood in Times Square. They had photographers, and it was almost surreal. They did a whole 'media tour' where they made several stops at different media outlets in New York City. It didn't seem like it was actually happening."

The band's music was tongue-in-cheek parodies of classic rock with newly-penned golf-related lyrics. For example, the Crosby, Stills & Nash song "Love the One You're With" became "Love the One You Whiff." (You can look that one up on YouTube.)

"They changed all the words, so they had to get permission from all the original artists to do these songs," Lisa remembers. "On the actual album that they recorded, they had whoever the artist was introduce their song." Artists included Alice Cooper, Hootie & the Blowfish, REO Speedwagon, and of course, Graham Nash and Steven Stills. "Now Mark has a radio show called *Time to Let It Fly*, which was the name of one of their songs."

Both Lisa and Mark have had some health issues, but that has only further cemented their commitment to each other. Lisa believes it's tougher to be the caregiver than to be the patient, because as a caregiver sometimes there is nothing you can do to help.

In 2002, the year Mark turned fifty, the melanoma in his leg returned after his being in remission for eleven years. That was a scary time. Lisa was already a devout Christian when she and Mark met, so it was natural for her to turn to her faith.

"There were times that I would go to church on my own when we would get home from trips," she says. "It wasn't something Mark necessarily wanted to do. But he had started going with me, probably for about six months, before he was again diagnosed with melanoma."

Mark's prognosis was uncertain. The day after receiving the devastating news, Mark went to church to pray and seek guidance. "At that point," Lisa says, "that's when he went on his own. I didn't know he had gone to the church that afternoon. He just sat at the altar."

His time at the church that day was filled with introspection and connecting with the Divine. He came away a changed man, having made a personal commitment to Christ.

Lisa was justifiably moved and comforted by this new direction. It was an amazing moment to have Mark come home to tell her he'd fully embraced the faith she'd been following all along. He had been afraid because of his diagnosis, and she had been afraid because of her love for him. His new perspective allowed them both to trust in something higher.

In the following months, Mark began a treatment plan of major surgery and intensive chemotherapy. He was able to resume broadcasting with the Golf Channel, and despite all the side effects from the treatment, he accepted an offer for a one-time exemption (meaning he wouldn't have to qualify) to play at his first tournament as part of the Champions Tour at the Senior British Open at Turnberry in Scotland (now that he was fifty), due to his status as a PGA Tour winner. With Lisa's full support, he went.

"Mark had always said, 'I will never play on the Champions Tour,'" Lisa says. "He had been playing competitive golf for so many years, through his whole junior career, college career, everything, that he was just done. But when he got that exemption, he was still doing his chemo. He had a new perspective on life at that point. And he thought, 'Let's just go.'"

Once there, Mark did face plenty of obstacles. Not only was he still undergoing treatment, he had diabetes to deal with, too. He had been diagnosed at age fifteen with type 1 and had lived with what that meant ever since. Lisa was worried about him, but wanted him to enjoy the amazing opportunity at Turnberry.

Mark had an incredible week with Lisa at his side. Not only did he make the cut, but he also played amazingly well. Lisa was proud of him as he walked all the hills of the course—a real challenge because of how badly his leg muscles had atrophied from the surgery and treatments. Even still, Mark's pain was sometimes evident. Lisa felt for him but was nonetheless cheering him on the only way she could. Astonishingly, Mark finished in the top 25 out of 144.

"He played so well that he ended up getting invited to all these other tournaments on the Champions Tour," Lisa says. "That's what spurred on the whole thing. He did that for about five years while still working on the Golf Channel." Thankfully, his cancer treatments were successful, and he is now again in remission.

The diabetes sometimes made being a golfer's wife especially challenging as Mark continued to compete. Lisa says it was hard on her when she couldn't be at tournaments with him. When she was not there, she did the next best thing and turned on her computer for the online live scoring that would be updated during tournaments at the time.

Lisa remembers one particular tournament Mark played in Baltimore when she was watching the scores online. He was scoring extremely well, and she was so excited for him, when all of the sudden he shot a bogey, and then two more bogeys after that. Lisa panicked at the computer.

"I didn't even know what was happening. Typically, if he had a bad hole or two or three, he would turn it around, but it wasn't happening. It was just getting worse. I just felt something was wrong." Lisa was sure that his blood sugar was dropping. But what could she do when she was so far away? "I did try to call him after the tournament was over and could not get ahold of him. He was doing TV immediately following, though, so I heard him on the air. That night, I finally talked to him, and he told me what had happened."

Mark's blood sugar had gone so low that he didn't even remember the last six holes. He was lucky that he didn't pass out on the course. Miraculously, he finished the round, but he withdrew from the rest of the tournament and came home. "Sometimes low sugars are very, very hard to recover from," Lisa says. "It takes a while. This one was so bad that he just wasn't feeling well. So, he came home the next day."

When Mark joined the Champions Tour players, Lisa became the new wife on the block. "Some wives are reserved and want to check you out, and others just accept you. It can be like high school all over again," Lisa says. But while most wives want their husband to win, if they are not a contender in a particular tournament, everyone freely roots for their friend's husband to win. Most of the players get along as well as the wives, so you are excited for them. Lisa says, "It's your family out there!"

If your husband has a great round, you may be celebrating with other golfers at the tournament and go out to dinner. But when the round doesn't go so well, you may be having a very quiet dinner in your small hotel room. When you are at home, you can at least go to some other part of the house for the necessary quiet time; in a hotel room, there is no place to hide. Lisa always gave Mark space and let him be. She sometimes tried to say something to make him feel better, but it took longer if it was a bad tournament versus just a bad round. Lisa is proud that no matter what the outcome of the round, Mark was always gracious. He gave countless autographs, even when the day didn't go his way. She says, "He is a good guy, through and through!"

In 2004, the tables were turned when Lisa was diagnosed with parotid gland cancer. This was very frightening because with the type of surgery needed, there's a risk of facial paralysis. Together Lisa and Mark researched the best facilities and doctors to treat this condition and chose Duke University Hospital. Thankfully, all went well. After the surgery in June, Lisa found out that a golf hole had been dedicated to her that day, at a practice round of the Bank of America Classic at Nashawtuc Country Club by the players, including luminaries like Jerry Pate, Andy Bean, Dana Quigley, and Craig Stadler (who won). Not only did Lisa's family and friends support her, but her extended golf family did as well. Lisa says, "I was told after I woke up from my surgery and was overwhelmed with emotion—so surprised. I was so touched that they cared and that they were all thinking of us and praying for us. It was beyond words. I felt like we were not alone."

During all of their trying times, Lisa and Mark's faith strengthened. Sometimes she would leave encouraging notes on his golf cart or put something in his golf bag. One of her favorites is Philippians 4:13, "I can do all things through Christ who strengthens me."

After being married for six years, Lisa and Mark had their first baby, Lucas, in 2005. Two years later in 2007, Eva arrived to complete the family.

"Our biggest blessing has been Lucas and Eva," Lisa says. "We had spent so much time, just the two of us. We were always on the road, always on the go, and it was really great. But I look back now, and I think it's almost like we were just spinning our wheels, filling time. The kids bring a whole new purpose into our lives. Mark has been such a good guide to them. I can't imagine life without them, and they've brought a whole new meaning to his life as well."

Having a baby when you are on the Champions Tour is like having a million instant grandparents. "I was definitely the only one out there pushing a stroller around the golf course," Lisa says with a laugh. "It was fun." The tour wives threw a baby shower for her, and they were so excited and welcoming when Lisa brought Lucas on the road with them. "Especially my good friend Soozi Pate [Jerry Pate's wife]—she just wanted to hold that baby. They made us feel very welcome."

Lisa is grateful for Mark's time on the Champions Tour. "The fact that I even got to be a part of any of that with him was amazing because I missed his time on the regular tour. I feel like it was just a huge bonus that I got to do that with him and to see him on a different level—to see him compete. It's almost like they have a different persona sometimes out there when they're competing."

Although it can look alluring from the outside, the golfing life has challenges like any other life. Lisa says, "Even just doing the TV and traveling, that's not at all glamorous. Sometimes it's the extreme opposite. But overall, it was a really, really great experience. I'm glad that I got to be a part of it with him. God has blessed us beyond my wildest dreams."

Even with the struggles they've had to deal with, Lisa and Mark are still very grateful. "Sometimes having struggles makes you realize how grateful you are when you don't have them. You appreciate the times when they're not there a little bit more."

Lisa purchased a curio cabinet a few years ago to store some of the special trophies Mark has won. The trophies were kept in boxes for years because of their moves, and Mark didn't want to make a shrine to himself. Lisa insisted on displaying them for their son and daughter. Mark relented, and it is a beautiful tribute to all of his hard work and talent.

Neither Lisa nor Mark ever wanted to force golf upon the children, but they did want to introduce it to them. When Lucas was a baby, he received a real golf club as a gift. Over the next few years, Mark purchased for the kids a putter, driver, and wedge. For some reason, Lucas didn't show much interest, but Eva had fun in their backyard of golf course grass with her mini set of clubs. Then the parents discovered why Lucas didn't like the sport so much. He said, "Daddy, golf takes you away." Now that Mark is mostly home after his retirement from the Champions Tour and Lucas is a teenager, golf is a sport they all share.

One of the funniest family stories involves golf carts. Lisa and Mark were in Chicago, and she was meeting him on the course. She was not familiar with the club, so she proceeded to the cart area and asked the person in charge which cart she could take. He told her to take any cart. Lisa jumped into the closest one and started driving toward the golf hole where Mark was waiting for her. As she drove two fairways over, she noticed people were staring at her and laughing. It wasn't until she reached Mark and his partner that she realized what she had done. Four golf carts were all connected, and she was driving a train! She was mortified, but had to take the carts back. When she returned the carts to the drop-off center, she casually said, "I only need one!"

When the children were small, Lucas and Eva enjoyed watching their dad on TV, both on the Champions Tour and when he served as a commentator. Lucas would say, "I wish Dad could talk back to me." Lisa loves that now the children can watch video of their father competing in golf at the highest level that he played in his prime. They have some film footage of the first Masters Tournament where he competed in 1984. Mark was playing extremely well, so he was on camera frequently. Lisa wasn't married to Mark at that time, but she is still the proud wife and impressed with his skills on the course.

Lucas is on the high school golf team, and since the team needed more players, they bumped up middle schooler Eva. With Mark as a coach, it's fun togetherness for the whole family.

Lisa has learned a lot about being supportive, even when what a player needs doesn't make logical sense. When Mark was still touring, she would carefully check to make sure he had his all-important three nickels. "A lot of players have these little—I guess they're kind of superstitions," Lisa explains. "Little things that they do. Mark's thing was he always had three nickels. They were the same three nickels for a long time, but when he lost one, he had to find another. If he was playing, he had to have three nickels in his pocket."

Lisa laughs off the superstitions that are rampant in golf. But, she admits, she has her own story to tell. "The funny thing now is I'm following Lucas and Eva. One time when we had regional tournaments, I found myself getting caught up in thoughts that have nothing to do with how they're playing, but you think they do. Mark wanted me to keep him posted about how Eva was playing, so I texted him that she was playing unbelievably great. But then I was like, *Oh my gosh, this golf course is super, super tough.* And then she went bogey, par, par, par, which was great for her. I thought, *Okay, I'll text him and let him know.* Well, right after I sent it, in my mind, I'm thinking, *Oh, the second I send that, something bad's gonna happen.*

"Then Eva triple bogeyed again. I texted Mark, 'I'm not sending any more texts,' with the laughing emoji—because it's ridiculous! I had to tell myself, *Her playing has nothing to do with what I'm sending out over the phone. It's just not related.* So, I kept texting." And Eva still did great.

Even still, Lisa was always helpful with Mark as far as his nickels went. She understood that a lot of the game is in the mind, and those nickels gave him confidence.

Eventually, Lisa began to see the effects that the constant grind was having on her husband. The idea of retirement always floated between them, but she knew that she couldn't tell him to stop playing the sport he loved. The choice had to be his.

"I could just tell everything was wearing on him," she says. "It was a lot to compete out there with guys who are practicing every single day. He was both starring on TV and trying to compete. It was just a lot. I left it up to him, but I did say, 'This is not adding anything to your life. We don't have to have it. You should stop, because if it's stressing you out, it's just not worth it.'"

At some point, Mark decided enough was enough. He went back to just doing the TV and seemed much happier after that. But the biggest transition was when he left the Golf Channel.

"He wasn't out at all the tournaments," Lisa says. "He wasn't traveling anymore. It took him a while to adjust to that. But now he's available to be a hands-on father."

Initially he started working at a golf course close by where they were members. The club had asked him to act as their director of golf, basically playing with incoming members or bringing new members on board. But it was his first time ever really having a boss. "I remember he came home one day," Lisa says with a laugh, "and he said, 'They actually want me to come in every day.' I said, 'Yes, hon, it's called a job.'"

Mark got used to that, but then started saying things like he'd retire completely at such and such an age. But Lisa isn't sure that will ever happen. "That's just not his personality," she says. "He has to be doing something. So even though he's not golfing anymore and is just doing strictly radio, it keeps him busy enough and involved still in golf, which is really good."

Lisa works to keep Mark from pushing too hard. "When you face the fear of losing someone, you can become pretty protective. He's very focused and driven. He would describe himself when he was younger as a very intense person, especially competing. I see he also has all these great softer qualities about him, too, but some people might not see that."

Then there's the aspect of protecting others from Mark. When

Mark is coaching the kids, for example, he has very high standards. "He's very intense with them because he wants to help them get better—more so with our own kids," Lisa says. "With any child whose parent is coaching them, it's probably a little more difficult versus getting instruction from a total stranger. I tell the kids, 'You know, Daddy's just trying to help you.' We were out in California one summer, and I met some of the guys he grew up with. They played high school and college golf together. I asked, 'What was Mark like when he was a kid like Lucas?' And his friend said, 'Oh, he was really intense. He was very focused.' Another guy said, 'My parents didn't trust any of my friends, but they trusted Mark.' He's kind of like an old soul or something."

The bottom line is that when you know what it takes to achieve a certain goal, you want to get those who also want to achieve it on the road to those skills as soon as possible. So, Lisa is sometimes the mediator between Mark and the world. "He expects people to go at it the same way he does," she says fondly. "And I'm like, 'You're unique, you know? Not everybody goes at it that way.'"

Now, life is a constant dance of teenagers, radio, and keeping their relationship strong. "The kids go to school," Lisa says. "Mark and I are both helping coach their golf teams. That's been life-consuming." Mark also has the radio show every Wednesday night, along with pregame and postgame shows over the weekend whenever there are tournaments going on. "When he does go out to the majors still," Lisa says, "he'll do four events on the road, so that keeps him busy enough. The great thing about the weekly show is he can do that out of our house. We set up a little studio, and he goes in there and does a show. It's a lot less travel than our former life. On most days when the kids come home from school, we go to the golf course, and then we come home, eat dinner, they do homework, and it starts all over again."

Lisa's day is not just about kids—she and Mark partner every day on organizing and executing the annual Lucas Cup. Founded by Lisa and Mark and named after their son Lucas, this newly relaunched pro-am event (featuring one pro in a group with four amateurs) benefits the Juvenile Diabetes Research Foundation. This organization's goal is to help those suffering with type 1 diabetes by continually doing research, working on life-changing therapies, and eventually finding a cure for this disease. Mark and Lucas are both type 1 diabetics.

Lisa wrote in her January 2020 blog entry on the Lucas Cup Foundation website, "As parents, we have so many dreams for our children. My dream is all of those, plus the dream of a cure. My dream is for Lucas to live a life to his fullest without the additional worries and physical ailments that are a result of diabetes. That is why I will exhaust myself in raising money to find a cure and to help educate others and support those who cannot afford insulin or supplies. That is why the Lucas Cup is returning this year. Will you help me help others?"

Lucas was diagnosed at four years old, and he's fifteen now. Making sure he's safe and healthy is the all-consuming commitment of his loving mother. What does that look like for Lisa? She explains, "That means I have an app on our phone so we can see his blood sugar all day long. If he goes high or low, an alarm will go off on our phone as well as his phone at school. At night, it's even more crucial and lifesaving. A typical diabetic does not wake up in the middle of the night when their sugar is low, which can be life-threatening. The good thing about this app is your alarm will go off to wake you up." That doesn't make everything easy, however. "My son very rarely wakes up even to a blaring alarm next to his ear," Lisa says. "So, I'm definitely up every night and just checking. I can't help it. For so many years, we were without that technology. I've always been used to waking up automatically to check on him. That's an every-night thing and an everyday thing."

This has tested Lucas as well. "He is very, very responsible and mature beyond his years," Lisa says, "so he stays on top of it very well. And seeing how well Mark takes care of himself, I think, is a huge, huge benefit to Lucas. Mark has been diabetic since he was fifteen, so he's had it for over fifty years. Of course, they had hardly any technology back then. It was just kind of guessing. So, he's done very well."

While the kids are in school for the day, Lisa works on everything that has to do with the Lucas Cup. It is a two-day pro-am with no less than twenty-six touring pros, with a Sunday night pairings party of 250 people and even a long-drive exhibition. "It's a huge endeavor," Lisa says. "The first four years we had it, we raised almost $2 million."

Lucas is in high school now, and Lisa is trying to plan ahead for when he leaves for college. "He'll have to take it on himself," Lisa says, with a tinge of worry in her voice. "That's when a lot of kids get into trouble with diabetes—when they go off to college. The lifestyle changes and their eating habits change. Everything changes. I'm a little nervous about that. We did get a dog. We're trying, although not super successfully as of yet, to train her to sense his sugar, or at least to react to his alarm. But I'm hoping the technology, which has been advancing pretty quickly, will have advanced enough by then so that we're closer to finding a cure before he leaves."

More changes loom for Lisa and Mark as both kids mature and head off for lives of their own. Lisa laughs and says, "I told Mark that after the kids leave, we'll find out how much we really like each other." But with a partnership that has spanned so much adversity along with so much joy, their foundation is strong. Lisa says, "We've been married for over twenty years and were together three years before that. I think we'll be fine."

4 Fun at the Club

Even though I love playing with Steve, at first I thought I wouldn't like playing with other couples because of my lack of golf skills. Then I learned about how couples' golf uses the handicap system—it was the first time my high handicap came in handy. With our golf scorecard full of my handicap dots (which translates to strokes subtracted on a particular hole), Steve and I actually had a chance to place in some of the couples' events.

Steve prides himself on being a pretty good coach. He's more than willing to instruct me as to how any shot should be played— especially when a match is on the line. Sometimes, it must be said, we disagree.

Not us, of course, but many husbands and wives have huge fights on the green. Most of the time, it's because many husbands want their wives to listen to their instructions. Many wives, on the other hand, simply do not like to be told what to do, nor do they like to be *mansplained* to death. It's understandable—after all, they have most likely been playing in their own women's leagues without their spouses and already fully know what to do. A few wives I know are actually better players than their husbands. But do they give advice? Not so much! Husbands, bless them, have been known to resist advice even more than their wives do.

"Honey, You Drive Me Crazy," one of my favorite couples' events, doesn't much help this situation. It is played by each person teeing off and then the partners have to take each other's drives. In my case, this is great because Steve can hit the ball at least 130 yards beyond mine. For Steve, this presents a wonderful, character-building opportunity to play the course very differently than he usually does. Suffice to say, he's usually not faced with the challenge of being so far from the pin.

The "Three Club Event" for couples is a challenge because you are only allowed three clubs and a putter to play the entire nine holes. This is not so hard for me—I have only a few favorite clubs anyway. Steve, though, likes to use all of his for the accuracy in getting right on the green and close to the pin. He knows within five yards what each club will do. I comfort him while we play with the assurance that this event is only once a year.

My overall favorite event is "Night Light Golf." We all get to the club around six o'clock to eat dinner, and then when it's dark outside, we head out. Each couple is handed three special golf balls that glow florescent green. We try to save the unused balls from year to year just in case we hit one into a pond. When they land in the pond, you can actually see them glowing on the bottom.

That night, the fairways are lined with glow sticks so you can see where to hit. It looks amazing—just like an airport runway. Even the flag sticks have glow-in-the-dark numbers. I remember one year, the couples' group before us forgot to put the flag stick back in the hole. Was that ever challenging—trying to hit a ball in total darkness into an unmarked cup. It always amazes me that, in the dark, someone does not end up in the pond with their golf cart. Club golf carts do not have headlights, but some of the privately-owned ones do. It can get tricky at this event to even see people, especially if they are not wearing a glow necklace.

After we are done playing, we head into the clubhouse for dessert, more drinks, and of course to hear who won the event. What a fun night!

After a few years of playing in the couples' events, Steve and I decided to be on the event organizing committee with some of our friends. I loved working with the club chef to plan all of the meals. I would design the menu to coordinate with the event. One year, for a Las Vegas–themed, couples'/guest-day event, we served surf and turf and even had flaming baked Alaska paraded into the ballroom. It was spectacular!

At that event, we also thought up the *Vegas-y* idea of dressing the head pro up like Elvis and having him stationed at a par-3 hole. When you got there, you would bet him who could get a better shot onto the green—and you got to choose his club (excluding the putter). Then you would hit as well, with the club of your choice. I lost my five dollars, but it was fun.

I usually try to be around for most of the couples' events, but one Friday night I happened to be in Florida. I phoned home, only to find out from my daughter Laura that Daddy was playing in the couple's event that evening! I'm thinking, *Just a minute.* Laura did not know any other details (or she wasn't saying), so I had to wait—patiently—until he got home to find out what was going on. Steve innocently explained that another member wanted to play in the event, and since her husband was out of town. . . etc. How convenient. Worse, she was a divorce attorney. I will admit that I was a little jealous—not because she was attractive, but because she was a better golfer than me. I was somewhat happy to hear that they did not win; otherwise, it would have messed with my psyche.

A few of our club members plan the *pièce de résistance* of the year: The Battle of the Sexes. You have to be invited to compete. They always ask Steve because he is such a competitive golfer—I get included only out of courtesy. I then politely and promptly decline; this is one event I want the ladies to win. And, as a spectator, I can drink and cheer the women on from the sidelines. As for supporting Steve, he gets my support the rest of the year. Oddly enough, over the years, this event has balanced out between the men and women winning.

The Battle of the Sexes starts with a potluck dinner at a member's house on Saturday, the evening before the scheduled event. After dinner and several cocktails later, the golf pairings are made based on handicap and a blind draw. It is fun to see who gets paired with whom. The partners then pair up again with another pair to form a team.

Early afternoon on Sunday, the contentious battle begins. Two of my good friends, Patty and Joan, always want to be paired with each other. They know how to cheer each other on, and they play well together. However, when Patty starts to play badly, she wants a drink in the worst way. Joan knows better than to let her drink before the round is over—once the drinking starts, it will never end. This motivation keeps Patty's head in the game. They almost always win their match, so I guess the strategy has worked for them.

It's a strategy everyone could learn from. Sometimes players will offer to buy their opponents drinks in order to get the edge up on their match, especially if they are playing badly. "Make it a double shot" is said to the beverage cart girls if the opponents foolishly accept. Other competitors try to play some head games by saying and doing irritating things that might affect their opponents. Whooping it up and hollering when making a great shot, then rubbing it in further with fist bumps often makes others a little tetchy if their shots are not going as well. "Sorry, your ball is in the water again!" is often said with a big smile. So irritating. Bad sportsmanship? Maybe. If so, we're all guilty. I can laugh—I'm on the sidelines.

There's another aspect of the match called "ham and egging it," when one person on a team does badly on a hole but the other does well. The good score counts, so that each teammate can save each other on a golf hole and still be competitive in the match. This happens with a lot of good partnerships, and it keeps everything fun.

As each team finishes, their results are posted on the big scoreboard for all to see. The crowd gathering on the patio overlooking the eighteenth hole gets larger and larger as teams finish. On our course, this hole is known for being the most difficult hole to putt. If you hit the ball too hard, it can go into a sand trap or totally off the green; if you strike the ball too softly, it can roll back down the hill. There are even a few undulations to make it even more unpredictable. With all that in mind and the growing crowd staring down from the terrace above, putting in the final minutes can be stressful. Maybe it's not a professional tournament, but the stakes are high in the Battle of the Sexes.

The crowd cheers—someone just sank their putt. You're done! You won (or lost) your round. Commence heavy drinking! Joan buys Patty a cosmopolitan for being good and not drinking on the course. Steve has joined me ages ago, and we are way ahead of them. Other members take their beverage of choice and head out on golf carts to check on the rest of the teams finishing up.

With more spectators watching, the pressure builds. One by

one the teams post their scores. Finally, we know whether it's the women or the men who get bragging rights for the next year. The losers are bummed out, but then they have more drinks, and soon everyone's laughing and having a good time. The prized trophy for winning after all this? A bright, monogrammed golf towel that says the year and proclaims them the winner in Battle of the Sexes. (The color changes every year.) This will be proudly clipped to the winning team's golf bags—until next time.

All of the events are massively fun. Steve and I truly delight in the camaraderie and competition, even if we don't win any pro-shop credits. Because they're at the club, no planning is necessary, and the meals are always extraordinarily delicious. It makes for an ideal date night. Not bad for old-time marrieds like us.

To add to the fun, almost all country clubs have "Guest Days." This is when a member can invite one or more guests to a planned event. The club gets the opportunity to roll out the red carpet (or, on a golf course, the green carpet), show off their facilities, and maybe recruit new members, too. It also gives the member a perfect opportunity to entertain friends, family, or clients. These are usually themed events and a lot of fun.

One year in October, I had foot surgery. Happy Halloween—it was no treat! It took six months to recover and finally wear normal shoes.

I couldn't play any golf that whole time. When a neighbor, Shirley, asked me once I was recovered to play in their club's guest day, I was reluctant, but I decided to commit. Our team included her daughter, Jan, and another neighbor, Yvette. We all drove over to the club together.

The guest day had a Jamaican theme. Many of the ladies dressed the part, with colorful Rasta turbans on their heads and beads. One lady had a fruit basket on top of her head. How on earth did she play golf in that elaborate costume? I had a challenging enough time just playing in my orthopedic-looking sandals. Our team wore powder-blue shirts and white skorts.

Shirley thought the eighteen-hole round would be a scramble, but it was not. In the end, they counted two best scores on the front nine and one best score on the back. That sounded like it would be a lot of golf for me, even more so because I hadn't played in six months. I was ready for some embarrassment!

I had never played golf with anyone in our group, so I was extremely nervous. Our foursome didn't even have time to warm up because we were too busy talking and eating breakfast. We finally found our starting hole, which was on the back nine. I got up to the tee to address the ball and took a fairly good swing. To my surprise, the ball went straight and even got some distance. Maybe the time away had done me some good, and for a change, I had forgotten my bad habits instead of my good ones.

I played pretty well on the entire back nine. We used several of my scores on the card. But once we continued on to the front nine, the other three ladies had to hold the team together. My mojo had vanished. Even still, when we finally finished the round, I knew we would be close to the winning score. It was a hot day, so we did our best to clean up in the locker room before lunch. I tried to hurry, as I was anxious to see the score board. Our team sauntered into the banquet room and paused at the scoreboard. Holy cow! We were only one point away from the winning score and took second place in our flight. I was thrilled—and ready for a cocktail.

Our prize was a fifty-dollar pro shop gift certificate. After lunch, we all went shopping. I found a lovely Kelly-green golf shirt with an Audubon Country Club logo to commemorate the victory. I'm glad the prize wasn't a trophy—trophies are just dust collectors. With Steve winning so often, I need to rent out mantel space at someone else's house.

For the past five years, Steve has played in a three-day guest tournament at our club with a good friend of his, Joe, who flies in from Chicago to play. They always have a great time, and the weather in Florida usually cooperates. On the final day of the tournament, they took second place and were only behind the winners by half a point. Their prize was a smaller version of the first-place trophy. It was a porcelain trophy in Wedgwood blue and white. Oddly enough, the top lifted off to reveal a little compartment. "Why not put it to good use and make it an urn for your ashes one day?" I joked with Steve. My humor is a little strange, since my father's side of the family has been in the funeral business since 1882. I told him I would have my brother store it for him at the funeral home. Why waste a good trophy?

A few weeks after my stellar performance, I was invited to play in another friend's guest day. I was feeling confident because of my previous win, so I said yes. It was at the beautiful Royal Poinciana Golf Club. I had never played this course and was looking forward to seeing it. The night before the event, my teammate Kathy Jo sent me a text asking if I wanted to dress alike. We wore bright-pink golf shirts with black skorts. I was thankful the request was normal golf attire and not some unusual costume!

The pristinely manicured grounds gave the club a stately feel. Once we arrived, we headed into the ladies' locker room, where refreshments were artistically arranged. There were lots of fancy pastries, fresh juices, and steaming-hot coffee waiting to be consumed. I bypassed the goodies and grabbed a glass of water en route to the driving range with Kathy Jo. We had never played golf together, so I didn't know what to expect. The guest day format was a two-person team scramble. Each of us would tee off, choose the best shot, and continue playing from the best location until the ball was holed out. Surely, I could handle that.

Lucky for us, Kathy Jo and I were the perfect team. Not only did our outfits match, but our handicaps were close, too. We received almost equal dots on our score cards—and you know how I love dots. They really help level the playing field. We were definitely ham and egging it, though. We took advantage of everything we could!

At the end of the round, I knew we had a great score. We tied for first place. Unfortunately, they did a blind draw to break the tie, and we drew second place. I was happy with the bragging rights, though, and the prize. There was no trophy to dust—it was a one-hundred-dollar spa gift certificate. Now, that is a prize. Kathy Jo and I decided we would make a day of it and celebrate our win. We went to the spa in the morning and had lunch afterward.

Over the years, I have attended and been a part of organizing many guest days. Sometimes coming up with a theme can be a real challenge. My club did an animal theme one year, and there were a lot of leopard-print shirts. That was the latest fashion that year, so they were easy to find. One club did a Las Vegas showgirl event. I did not play in it but saw a picture of how one team dressed up. The four women wore very tall headpieces, fishnet tights, and even skimpy leotards. It's too bad they didn't have a prize for the most creative costume. I know those girls didn't play well in their outfits, but they sure had people smiling.

Guest days are always fun and entertaining, even if your score is high. Both Steve and I love being invited to a guest day, and it's our pleasure to invite guests to our club for these incredibly fun events. The scrumptious meals, the fancy alcoholic libations, and the camaraderie usually make you forget a poorly played round. It's extra frosting on the cake when you win or place in the event. Although the prizes range from the premium, like a spa day or pro shop credits, to the poor, like a silver bowl that tarnishes, it's the recognition of the achievement that makes a person feel special.

So, when the golfer in your life suggests that maybe it's time to join the club, fear not. It could be a great time. The overall best things about club membership are the camaraderie among friends and meeting new and interesting people who share in the bond of golf. And who knows, you may get some bragging rights!

5 Golf 101

Ask any New Yorker: When someone asking for directions says, "How do I get to Carnegie Hall?" (as the old joke goes), a New Yorker will answer, "Practice, practice, practice." Same goes for golf. Granted, some fortunate people are gifted or are just natural athletes. But for those of us who are normal humans, we must practice till it hurts.

My first venture with golf started with my husband teaching me the basics. Surprisingly, we're still married. Between working with a professional coach or with a professional marriage counselor, the choice was simple—and ultimately, less expensive. Once Steve admitted I needed more help than he could give, our neighbor Mary suggested that she and I share lessons at her golf club, Edgewood Valley. That way we would save a little money and get some extra practice time in as well.

I liked the instructor. He made it fun and was good at getting me to actually make contact with the ball on a consistent basis—truly an accomplishment. We stuck with him for a few months until Mary adopted a baby. Golf and babies do not mix. Typically, a round of eighteen holes takes about four hours and twenty minutes.

On a bad day, I could easily go five hours chasing that little white ball around. Hauling around the golf clubs is bad enough—try playing the links with a stroller and a crying baby inside.

My next venture with lessons was at Kemper Lakes when we were there on vacation. Steve signed us up for a *Golf Digest* Golf School. The weather was miserable, rainy, and unseasonably cold. I called the school to see if we could reschedule, but they had a no-refund policy. Lessons were an indulgence for us at the time. We were not willing to lose $400.

So, off we went. We drove an hour to get to the course, and the weather did not improve. Once we arrived, the two of us headed to the driving range to meet our first instructor, Roy. One of the other four people in the class had broken his wrist the week before, and even he showed up. That's the power of no refunds.

Roy quickly assessed a person's swing, made a few adjustments, and moved on to the next person. When you take group lessons, I learned, your time with the instructor is limited. Just because you need the most help doesn't mean the instructor can stay with you the whole time. Roy moved on, and I had to deal with my inconsistent swing by myself.

Thank goodness we had worn our rain gear. Steve and I were both fully dressed in waterproof pants, jackets, and hats. (We weren't making any fashion statements, just being smart!) The slight drizzle from that morning had now turned into a downpour, and the temperature was in the low sixties. I was freezing and miserable, but that lesson went on, come hell or high water. We took a break at noon for lunch. I couldn't believe we had hit balls for three hours in the rain. Hot soup and hot chocolate took the edge off. (I could have used a double shot of Bailey's in mine, but unfortunately that wasn't an option.)

At one o'clock we met our next instructor, Amy, to go over pitching, chipping, and sand shots. The rain had subsided, and I was elated. Amy had us do a few drills. We would practice and then move on to the next skill. Eventually, we headed over to the sand traps. Amy hit a few balls out of the four-foot-deep sand trap with ease. Then she had us move to the opposite side of the sand trap so that we could not see her swing. She told us to watch the area. Sand flew out, and so did the ball. When we came back to the other side, she gave us the best tip of the day: "If you can't get out of the trap, throw the ball with one hand and a handful of sand with the other!" She was joking, but it was the most useful thing I learned that day. I just had to remember to make sure the other players were out of sight. Before you ask, no, dear reader, of course I have never done that for real—unless I was playing with Steve.

Soon it was our turn to practice hitting out of the sand. Hitting a ball out of a dry sand trap can be a challenge, but when it's wet, it's a nightmare. It's close to impossible unless you don't take any sand. However, you want to hit some sand along with the ball to control where the ball lands. This is critical when you are close to the pin. If you don't take any sand, you will most likely hit over the green and be in trouble again. You must take sand, even when it is packed down from the rain.

At that point in the lesson, the only sand I was interested in was on a beach somewhere tropical. Every swing I took was killing my arm. I felt like I was striking my club against a cement wall. After about thirty swings, I practiced the instructor's desperate move of sand and ball throwing. Success!

A round of golf on the course was included in our lesson package for that day. Do you think after practicing golf six hours in the rain, I had the energy to play eighteen holes? But of course,

Steve asked. I answered with a definite, "Hell no! Are you crazy?" Even without the rain, I would have been sapped of the stamina by then. But Steve persisted, and of course I caved. "Okay, we can try the front nine."

Steve and I were the only ones playing; the rest of our class bailed. I think they were the only ones with brains. At least it stopped raining. We had the course to ourselves, which was pretty special. Sure, I was tired and feeling achy. If it hadn't been for the love of my husband and his love of the game, I would not have been able to keep going. We had completed eight holes when the skies opened up again, and the torrential rains came. It was a race in the cart to the clubhouse. I was freezing and soaked. They told us we could come back and play the other nine holes at a later date. I knew that wouldn't happen.

It took me a few days to recover from that ordeal. My body finally thawed out, but my left elbow still ached from hitting out of the wet sand trap. Golf lesson #237: don't hit out of compacted sand or extremely tall grass—it's better to take the one-stroke penalty and get out of the danger zone. My left knee was also aching. Even Steve wanted me to do something about it. I finally relented, and he took me to see my orthopedic surgeon, Dr. Henry Fuentes. An MRI showed another large tear in the meniscus in my elbow and damage in my knee. My medical chart is like an encyclopedia of orthopedic issues. Golf sure can wreak havoc on your body.

The surgeon scheduled a double procedure for the following week. I asked if I could get a two-for-one deal. Dr. Henry laughed, but I didn't. He said he would start at the knee and scope it, then work next on the elbow with a more invasive procedure. This meant a bigger incision—another battle scar worn with pride.

Steve was very supportive. He took notes and asked questions.

I was overwhelmed with the idea of having my entire left side not functioning. The double surgery did make sense because if you have one ache and pain, you won't be bothered by the second, or vice versa. Recovery time would be the same, so being a couch potato for a few weeks and having Steve as my nurse would be okay. Steve was concerned but was confident in the skills of our good friend, Dr. Henry. He asked so many questions that day. As for me, I just wanted the entire ordeal to be over.

On the day of the surgery, I woke up with some nervousness—it was my stomach, and it was saying, "Feed me." Unfortunately, before surgery you can't eat or drink (no alcohol, of course, and no water either). For this reason, I try to request the first surgery of the day. I do not mind being at the hospital or the surgical center at 6:00 a.m., although Steve is not happy about that hour. Being the amazing husband that he is, though, he never complains about that. It also gives me more time to recover from the anesthesia, which sometimes is a problem for me. Sometimes I have been the last patient out of a day surgery center. Steve earns his angel's wings with his patience sitting by me with a book or a golf magazine in hand. I always pray for an easy surgery and a quick recovery, as the down time is monotonous.

Dr. Henry walked in the room as I was getting prepped. We joked a little, and then he took out his marker and put an X on the correct spots for the surgeries. I can only imagine what kind of episodes in medical history led to adding that to standard procedure.

Both procedures went well, and the recovery and therapy took about six months. What is the saying? "For the love of the game"? The follow-up appointments on both my knee and elbow showed that I was making progress. My problem was that I expect too much from myself and want to be good as new the next day.

Steve was a gem, and his nursing skills had improved since my earlier surgery. I required more help this time getting around, and some basic skills presented a challenge. Steve was not used to washing long hair, but together we came up with a plan that would work. Since my arm was in a sling and my leg in a wrap, our long kitchen counter by the sink provided a space where I could lie and get the beauty shop treatment. With the addition of a thick beach towel down to cushion the hard surface, my kitchen spa was created. Getting up there was not like climbing Mount Everest, but it did require a step stool, a chair, and Steve's strong arms. Once up on the counter, I could relax and enjoy the spa-like shampoo. Steve was good at massaging shampoo in and not spraying water all over the kitchen. It felt wonderful to have clean hair.

I didn't play golf for the rest of the season. It was surprisingly easy to get used to being a couch potato. There were no early-morning tee times to rush out for, and I could sip that second cup of coffee. I was good as new for the next year. It was tough, but I learned to pay better attention if I felt an ache or pain. A body part can last a lot longer if you take care of it.

My next venture with lessons was in the winter with a friend of mine, Mary. She was a member of Crystal Tree and in the nine-hole golf league, too, and she agreed to come down to meet me after Steve and the other members of the executive branch finished a business trip to Naples, Florida. The group's wives were invited. I gladly accepted in order to escape the freezing Chicago weather in February and get some time in the sun, and it would be fun to hang out with Mary afterward. The La Playa Hotel was charming and in the perfect location, right on the beach.

The business trip flew by with the men having meetings all morning and playing golf in the afternoon. The wives would meet for breakfast to plan out our day. We spent a few days shopping and a few days soaking up the Florida sunshine on Vanderbilt Beach. It was a heavenly trip because the weather up north was snowy and bitter cold. Back home, the kids were enjoying their grandparents and going out for dinner at their favorite places every night. We were doing the same with the amazing cuisine in downtown Naples. (I think the menus were somewhat different!)

The business trip ended for my husband on Sunday, and slowly the group disbanded and headed to the airport. Everyone had different flights because they did not want the company executives all on one plane. (In case it crashed! Reassuring!) Steve's cab to the airport was one of the last to leave. I stayed on to go to golf school with Mary, who would drive from Daytona Beach after visiting family.

I walked with Steve through the hotel lobby and down the stairs to say goodbye. I felt so sad that he was leaving. Tears started slowly trickling down my cheeks. I kissed him and hugged him for as long as I could. Steve finally said he had to go, and I unclenched my arms from around him. You would have thought I was sending him to war. I'm not sure why I was so emotional. Heck, I would see him again in five days. Mary would be arriving by dinner time from Daytona, so I wouldn't be alone for long. Was I freaked out about the golf lessons, or did I anticipate missing my husband? I think a little of both.

I went back to my room quickly, not wanting to run into anyone with my teary eyes. I looked out the window at the beautiful Gulf of Mexico and thought, *Everything will be okay!*

Mary got there around six. I felt relieved when she arrived and knew we would have fun. We ate dinner in the hotel restaurant overlooking the Gulf. The sun had now set, and the sky was a gorgeous shade of orange intermixed with pinks and purples. That night we had a pajama party in her room and watched a little TV before getting the necessary *zzz*'s for the three-day golf clinic.

The next day arrived. I put on the outfit I had picked out the night before for my first lesson. As I've said, if you can't play well, at least you can look good. Mary and I had a quick breakfast and drank the necessary caffeine to wake up. I hadn't slept very well and was nervous about the lessons. The weather had gotten colder, which didn't make me any happier.

We arrived at the beautiful LA Playa Golf Club and dropped our clubs off at the bag drop. *What did I get myself into?* I asked myself. Our instructor seemed nice enough. He definitely looked the part. He was about forty-five years old, six feet tall, and slim.

We were waiting for one more person to join the group. In walked Billy, a tall, athletic guy with blond hair that curled up on the back of his neck and a megawatt smile. He gave us all a friendly handshake. It turned out Billy was a well-known local country western singer.

We headed out to the driving range in our golf carts. Our clubs were already at the range, ready to go. I wish I could have said the same about me! I did a little stretching and then picked up my 8 iron and began swinging. Once again, I was clearly the worst golfer in sight. But then again, if I were good, why would I be taking lessons?

All three of us kept hitting the range balls. The instructor would help us individually by making adjustments to our swings. He did this for an hour or so and videotaped us as well. That way, we could review our before and after swings and see the improvements.

Billy had a fairly good swing and wanted to improve his game for future professional/amateur tournaments. Mary and I just wanted to improve for our league and self-esteem. At noon, we took a break for lunch and warmed up from the chilly weather. It had stayed overcast and in the mid-sixties. Mary and I knew what we had to do after that day's lessons — shop for warmer clothes for the next day!

After the delicious lunch, we headed back to the range to be introduced to a contraption known as the "swing arc." It looks like a giant vertical hula hoop. When you use it as you swing, it guides your club in place so that you learn the correct swing path, helping your body commit the feel to memory. It worked great for me — while I was using it. The problem was, it was too big to take home in my golf bag. My body, apparently, has a bad memory. The frustration never ends.

The lesson was over at four, and Mary and I were both exhausted. But before we could crash, we had to shop for some warmer golf clothes. The next two days were going to be even colder. I was beginning to think there was a correlation between golf lessons and bad weather.

The second day was more fun because I knew what to expect. My golf swing improved significantly, and I was feeling more confident. I just wished it were warmer.

That day we worked on chipping and putting. I enjoyed the putting because that is one area in which I have always been fairly good. Our family used to play a lot of miniature golf when I was growing up, and all that "practice" paid off when putting. The saying is, "You drive for show, but you putt for dough!" Although I wasn't winning any money that day, I felt proud when I sunk some of the longer putts.

The next morning on the golf course, I was almost sad that our lessons were coming to an end. It was fun with the three of us; I actually enjoyed the lessons and the company. The last day included a round of golf on the course after the final lesson. Mary, Billy, and I all decided to test our newly-acquired skills.

It was a fun round. I couldn't believe the improvement in my game. I know the hard, flat Florida ground helped my ball roll a little farther, but my accuracy on driving and chipping had improved as well. I was feeling relaxed—and the drinks we had at lunch to celebrate helped, too. I was shocked after we added up the scores that I'd actually shot a 104. That was my all-time best score for eighteen holes at that point.

After the round, we stopped by the pro shop to pick up our golf videos. Mine would serve as a good tool to review in case I went back to my old bad habits. Once home again, that year in the nine-hole league, I won the trophy for "Most Improved Golfer"!

If golf came easy, more people would be playing. I have heard from so many people over the years who tried to play and just gave up. They could not improve their skill level enough to keep them motivated. That's why golf/sport psychologists—and the nineteenth hole—have a steady business.

To keep improving as a golfer, coaching and lessons are a must. The real challenge is to be consistent. One day you could be good with your driver but your putting stinks, making you score badly. The very next week, it could be the total opposite. Do you go for a putting lesson, or do you take a lesson with your driver? Either way, it's a necessity to practice, practice, and practice!

ROLE PLAY: JAN JACOBSEN

Not every golfer's wife has to go through this initiation. Take Jan Jacobsen, for example. Jan grew up playing golf. She never remembers a time when she herself didn't play and practice to become good at the game. Born in Portland, Oregon, she was one of five children. Her family belonged to Riverside Golf and Country Club, where her father encouraged her to take up the sport. She played in many tournaments herself as an amateur.

To hear Jan tell it, being married to a professional golfer is different than being married to someone who plays golf avidly but not for his job. Her cousin's husband, a stockbroker, would drive his wife to distraction by going straight from his office at the end of the day to the golf course and staying there until dark. Jan, married to Peter Jacobsen (professional golfer and commentator on the Golf Channel and NBC), understands why this could be frustrating. But she says, "When Peter's at the golf course, he's at his office. That's his job!"

Peter has played on the PGA Tour and the Champions Tour. He has won seven events on the PGA Tour and two events on the Champions Tour, both majors. But Jan says, if Peter spent all day and all night at the golf course and then went from there to the gym or anyplace else and didn't come home, she'd have a problem with that, too.

Jan's brother Mike, a professional golfer, first introduced Jan to Peter (also from Portland) when she was eighteen. Mike originally tried to fix Peter up with Jan's best friend. However, when Mike was flipping through some pictures in his wallet, Peter noticed Jan.

"Who is that?" Peter asked.

"It's just my sister," Mike replied with a shrug. But Peter continued to show interest.

Then, one day, Jan was set to play in an amateur tournament in Southern Oregon and needed to work on her bunker shots. She asked Mike for some help, but he took the opportunity to play matchmaker and pretended to be busy. He set her up with Peter for the lesson. The two discovered they were both students at University of Oregon (the Ducks, not the Beavers), he a sophomore, she a freshman. Sparks flew, and soon, they were a couple.

Peter did not plan to be a professional golfer, but his game improved significantly in college so he wanted to try. Jan was always supportive. She understood the game and, because of her brother, knew a lot about the tour. And she herself continued to compete. In fact, during their time in college, usually it was Peter having to travel when Jan had a special event with her sorority. However, one time the tables were reversed when Peter's fraternity had an overnight house dance at Oregon's Crater Lake. This was a big to-do, and amazingly, Peter had no conflicts. He asked Jan to go. She had to turn him down; she had her own golf tournament that weekend. However, she also let him know in no uncertain terms that he was to go stag: "You're not taking some other girl to an all-night party."

Jan and Peter married during winter break of her senior year on December 28, 1976. She was twenty-one years old and had one more semester to go to complete her degree in recreation. Peter had finished school the semester before their wedding and was playing in some mini tours in Phoenix, which typically consisted of four to six events. The contestants' entry fees made up the purse. When Peter tried to qualify those first two weeks of 1977 in Phoenix and Tucson, Jan was there. Unfortunately, he did not make either cut. She hung out in their junky hotel while he practiced. Despite it all, they had fun. That was their honeymoon!

Jan flew back to school, and then Peter qualified for the Bing Crosby National Pro-Am Tournament, which was his first. She called her dad and asked him to buy her the ticket to fly down to Pebble Beach, which he did. To save money, Jan and Peter stayed with a sorority sister of hers. It was a tiny place, and they slept on a sofa bed.

Playing the tour was challenging back then because, unlike other sports (for example, football or basketball) where the organization would take care of you, with golf tournaments at that time, you just showed up. No one provided information about which hotels were close to the golf courses, and of course, in the late 1970s, there was no internet. Jan was once stuck sitting in a hotel room reading and eating only a chocolate candy bar for lunch. If friends were there, it was more fun; otherwise, it was boring until the tournament started.

Even though it was up to the pro golfers or their spouses to find a place to stay, Jan had no idea how to proceed when Peter gave her that assignment in Philadelphia. Perplexed, she spoke to one of the other wives, who graciously gave her a list of convenient hotels that she had put together. The list even included the price ranges. This was a lifesaver for Jan, and she only wished it had happened prior to halfway through the year.

When Jan began traveling on the tour with Peter, the Byron Nelson tournament took place at Preston Trail Country Club in Dallas. It was an all-men's club, so women were not allowed to set foot in the clubhouse. Instead, the club provided a trailer outside for the wives. In the trailer, a few volunteers served muffins and fruit.

Jan walked into the trailer and found a place to sit with the book she was currently reading. (She was never without reading material.

It gave her something to do until the tournament started.) She did not know many people at the time, so walking into a room full of strangers was a little intimidating. More wives finally entered the trailer. Jan kept her nose in her book, but in reality, she was trying to figure out who they all were.

Finally, another girl came into the trailer, said hi to everybody, and immediately noticed Jan. "I don't think I've met you," she said. "I'm Beth Rogers." Jan introduced herself. "Oh," Beth said, "you're Peter's wife." Then a couple of others responded with, "We know Peter; he's so nice."

Jan was grateful to Beth for breaking the ice. They are still friends to this day. Jan says it always worried her that she would forget someone that she had already met or not remember their name. Now, the PGA Tour puts on the AT&T annual new-wives luncheon for newcomers to meet long-timers. It makes everyone feel welcome.

Jan's never being without a book became legendary. Mike "Fluff" Cowan was Peter's caddie for many years, and Jan also utilized his services—especially to avoid having to lug a book around the golf course when Peter was playing. Instead, she would hand her book to Fluff on the first tee to put in Peter's golf bag. One time in the late 1970s, she showed up with the bestseller *Shogun*, an extremely hefty novel at over eleven hundred pages. Fluff took one look and said, "Not in this bag." After that, she never heard the end of it. How big was her book this time? Would it make the bag too heavy?

Out of all Peter's tournaments, the first that he won, back in 1980, is the most memorable for Jan—but not for the reason you might think.

By then, three years into Peter's golf career, Jan and Peter had started their family with daughter number one, Amy, born just five weeks prior in Portland. Peter was home for the delivery and there for two weeks, but then he had to leave to continue the season. Jan planned to stay home, but she didn't enjoy being without him, even with her own mom nearby and helping her. Jan says, "I called him and said, 'Okay, I'm not really liking being by myself with this baby all night.'" The doctor cleared her and the baby for travel, so she was soon on her way to the Buick Open in Michigan.

Jan assured Peter that the baby was already sleeping most of the night, but she forgot about the time change—a big mistake! "When I got there, we couldn't get her to bed till two o'clock in the morning," Jan remembers. "The next night we got in the car with her and drove around till we got her to go to sleep." By now Peter was feeling the effects of interrupted sleep, and he was concerned about doing well in his last round. He said to Jan, "I don't know what we were thinking having a baby! How are we ever going to do this?"

Another golfer and his wife, Phil and Kitty Hancock, came to the rescue. They had a little one-year-old, so they had booked a two-room suite. They offered to let Peter sleep in their second room, with their more cooperative baby sleeping peacefully in the crib. "And he wins the tournament!" Jan says. There were other tournaments that were also meaningful for different reasons, but that one was critical to their going forward as a family.

It has turned out that having family close makes Peter's game stronger. He likes it when he knows where everybody is; he is much more relaxed. Back then, it was especially hard to be away from his family out on the road. Most of the time, when he wasn't playing, it could feel very empty. As Jan and Peter's family grew to include daughter Kristen and son Mickey, they worked hard to figure out the best way they could spend as much time together as possible.

One of the many decisions that professional golfers face is

whether or not to move if the family is not centrally located for the tour. Portland, Oregon, is about as far from tournament terrain as you can get. But together, Jan and Peter decided that it was more important to raise the children with their respective families nearby. They chose to keep Portland as their home base.

Because the children were all so close in age, traveling was a challenge. Jan wouldn't do it alone often. She would do it with Peter, or she would bring their babysitter from the neighborhood. By the time Amy was ready for school, choosing where she should go loomed as a huge decision. In the end, Jan and Peter still decided to stay in Portland. All the children went to school there. To balance this, Jan and Peter also made it a goal to not be apart for longer than three weeks. If Peter couldn't get home, Jan would pack up the kids and go to him. Sometimes she would even take the kids out of school. It wasn't easy to keep the family in Portland. They got creative and made it work. In the end, both Jan and Peter are glad that the kids know their extended families the way they do.

One of the ways Jan coped with the frequent separations was to set a standard Peter had to meet. As she tells it, "I did say to him, 'Look, you can go do whatever you want. I just need you to call me every night, and you have to listen to my boring stories about what the kids did that day.'" Now, of course, there are cell phones and texting and even video chatting that make staying connected that much easier. Back then, it was all about appointment conversations.

It was just as hard being on the other end of separation for Peter. When he was on the road and he couldn't get in touch with Jan, this caused some anxiety. If Jan wanted to take the kids to the park or go grocery shopping, but that was the only moment Peter had available, he would find himself calling and calling and getting no answer. Finally, out of desperation, he'd call Jan's mother to try

The Golfer's Wife

to find her. He explained later that it wasn't that he cared what she was doing; it was that he was lonely sitting up there in some hotel, and he knew he'd be unable to call soon because he had to leave.

"You know, it was really hard," Jan says. "I understood that. So, I said, 'All right, here's what I'm going to do. From now on, if I'm leaving the house, I will call my mother and say where I'll be. That way, Peter always had some place he could call." This was only when the kids were very young, and it was pre-cell phones. There was no way to speak with each other unless he was physically in his hotel room and she was at home. The golf tour may seem glamorous, but, Jan says, "It doesn't mean it's easy for the guys. Sure, they're out there doing what they absolutely love and want to be doing, but do they love being on the road? No."

Jan also made the unconventional decision to arrange to be able to take Amy (and later, her other children) out of school on a moment's notice. "I felt it was just as important for our children to be a part of Peter's life on tour as it was for them to be in school," Jan says. "The more we went out with him, the more we were comfortable with that life and became part of that. We could talk to him about it when he came home." The family gained memories they could all share of being at certain tournaments together. "It wasn't as much of a separation."

Other families made the choice to homeschool their kids so they could be on the road the entire time. This wouldn't have worked for Jan. "I asked the kids, 'What do you guys think about that? Would you ever want to do something like that?' And they just started laughing. I said, 'What's so funny?' and they replied, 'You're not smart enough to teach us, Mom.'" Jan laughs about it now. "End of discussion." Her grown children now include a vice president of marketing and communications, a neurologist, and a lawyer, so she figures they were probably right.

As the children grew into adolescence, Peter had to make some choices, too. His favorite tournaments of the year were down in California (Pebble Beach and San Diego) because at least they are on the West Coast. But Mickey was playing high school varsity basketball during his senior year in 2002/2003, right when those tournaments were held. Jan says, "I told Peter, 'It is his varsity year. I think you're going to be sorry if you don't see these games.' Peter just wasn't used to thinking that way because the tour was his job."

Different golfers have different times of the year and different courses that just fit their game. The tournaments in question were at the beginning of the season, and Peter always started out really strong. That was when he played his best. It was hard for him to say he wasn't going to play those tournaments that he looked forward to the most. But there was no argument about it. "As soon as I pointed it out," Jan says, "he stopped a minute. He was like, 'Oh my gosh, you're right.' And that was it. Now I say, 'Do you miss those couple of tournaments that you didn't play?'"

Jan also tried to attend as many tournaments as she could. She got close to many of the other golfers' wives that way. When husbands are paired in a tournament, the wives often walk the course together and follow them. The only time that can be stressful is on the tournament's last day if you're in the last group. Before that, Jan thinks that if the whole group plays well, it's better. It gets the golfers going. Obviously, you want your husband to win. However, you're never wishing bad things for the other players, many of whom have become your dear friends.

Jan remembers the PGA Championship in 1986 at Inverness Country Club, when it did get awkward. Peter was in the last group paired with Bob Tway and Greg Norman. Tammie Tway, Laura

Norman, and Jan, all good friends, were walking together. The last round seemed to be very up and down. Most of the day it appeared that Greg Norman was leading. Jan remembers that it was maybe on hole #10 that someone hit a ball left, and it went off the fairway and landed under a tree—disaster. After that hole, the ladies drifted apart and walked separately just because they were all so tense. It was a major tournament, so it was a big deal.

Then Peter's game took an unfortunate turn, and Jan knew he was not going to win. It could have then gone either way between Bob and Greg, but Greg had the better chance of winning. Greg's wife Laura separated off from their trio as things got more suspenseful. Jan and Bob's wife, Tammie, sat next to each other on the eighteenth hole. They were both thinking Greg was going to win, so they had relaxed a little. But then Bob Tway holed it out of a sand trap to win the tournament. Bob jumped up and down in the sand trap, and Tammie's eyes brimmed with tears of joy.

Jan was happy for her friend, but at the same time she always felt sadness when her own husband didn't win. "There's a small number of golfers who win a lot of tournaments. There's a bigger group who win, but don't win all the time. Peter is definitely in that group. It is a huge deal to win. His first win was amazing. Once you've got that under your belt, there are so many things that change," Jan says.

While many golfers find losing to be very difficult, Jan is fortunate that Peter rolls with the highs and lows of the game. Peter's generally a very happy, positive person. Even when he has a bad round, it doesn't ruin his whole night. But back in the day, Jan would still try to be helpful. Finally, he told her what he really needed.

"I was probably trying to talk to him right afterwards," she remembers, "and he said, 'Just give me a half hour. Let me just stew about it on my own. Don't talk to me. Let me just process it all, and then I'll be fine.'"

Jan has since told quite a few younger golf spouses that same story. It's natural to feel bad about a spouse having a challenging round, and it's easy to think you need to say just the right thing to help them feel better. But, as Jan now knows, it's best to leave Peter to his own processing. "What he needed was just not to hear me talk," she says. "Usually he would go into the locker room or something like that, and I would stand outside with his caddie and chitchat for a while." Peter would work it out himself and come out in a better head space.

One of the most exciting opportunities that came from Peter's becoming well known was his appearance as himself in the Kevin Costner golf film, *Tin Cup*. "That was really fun," Jan recalls. "The kids and I walked with Peter the whole time. The girls got to stand along the fairway in one of the scenes, and Ron [director Ron Sheldon] asked Mick [then about eleven] if he would run up to his dad." Mickey even had a speaking line, and then gave Peter a big hug.

Mickey was so excited that he told all his friends he was going to be in the movie. But when the family went to the premiere in Los Angeles, they discovered that the scene had been cut. "They decided to replace it with a [golfer] Craig Stadler scene—and in all honestly, it was much funnier," Jan says. She did go to the director afterward and mentioned that he really should have told them ahead of time. Shortly afterward, Ron Sheldon sent the family footage of Mickey's scene to show his buddies. They had a *Tin Cup* party at their house with all of Mickey's friends to see the original "alternate ending."

There's sometimes a downside, though, to all the attention. When Peter was playing with Jack Nicklaus in a US Open in 1996, everybody had been talking about it being Jack's last US Open. But Jack had assured Peter earlier that day that this wasn't going to be his last. At the end of the round on the eighteenth hole, Jack motioned for Peter to walk up there with him. The crowd was clapping for Jack, but Peter was right up there with him.

Some people in the audience got upset that Peter didn't hang back and let Jack have his supposed "final US Open" moment. A week or two later, son Mickey, then about twelve, was in the crowd at the Western Open and overheard two men saying that, due to the US Open episode, Peter was a "jerk." They even said other unkind things, like "I hope he doesn't make his putt." Mickey got more and more upset with each nasty thing they were saying. He found Jan for comfort, and she explained what had transpired that time between Jack Nicklaus and Peter.

At the end of the round, Mickey told Peter about the two guys. Jan said to Peter, "Forget about it." But Peter insisted on finding the men. Mickey pointed them out. Peter quickly made a beeline in their direction and said, "I hear you have a problem with me." Peter said that his son had overheard them. He then further explained that it wasn't Jack's last US Open, and that Jack asked him to be up there. Jack didn't want people to think it was his last round.

The guys apologized, and Peter told them they needed to be more careful when talking about people in a crowd. Jan was about to die of embarrassment, but Peter wasn't about to let it go—not when his son was involved. He made his point—but he was nice about it.

As Peter's career developed, he leveraged his achievements as a player into business and broadcast success. His Peter Jacobsen Sports, a full-service sports and entertainment marketing firm, was founded in 1989. He has been a presenter for two shows on the Golf Channel. A self-taught guitarist, Jacobsen was a founding member and lead singer of Jake Trout & The Flounders, a band he formed in the mid-1980s with good friends Mark Lye, Payne

Stewart, and Larry Rinker. The group is no longer together, but they recorded two albums. Their second album was released in 1999, with Times Square providing the memorable setting.

"Peter has a lot of energy," Jan says. "He is not someone who's going to go play golf and come home and just sit there. He's constantly thinking of things. I mean, really constantly." Even though he loves to be home for extended periods, she can tell that he sometimes gets "antsy" if there's not enough going on. That's when he'll suggest a new adventure. Jan happily goes along. She laughs. "He's sixty-five—maybe it'll slow down pretty soon."

Jan wishes she could play more golf, but other priorities have taken over. Some home remodeling and travel back and forth between Florida and Oregon has been very time consuming—and tiring. With an extended family and elderly parents, Jan has her own very full plate. Grandchildren have started coming, though, which is wonderful. Jan says, "It's hard to think of anything else besides wanting to see them."

She also manages Peter's expenses and is his first sounding board for ideas. She says, "He did say to me just recently, about our brainstorming, 'That's you.' I am definitely a part of his process in all these things he does. I enjoy being a part of that process. I'm not a good number one. I'm a good number two."

Jan believes that it's critical for the "number one" to have a partner at their side who is creatively supportive. If she were going to give advice today to anyone linked with a highly active, well-known professional, she'd say, "There's only room for one rooster in the henhouse."

She herself almost made the mistake in the beginning, even before children, of thinking she didn't need to be so connected to Peter's work. But her own father set her straight. "I came home one time from a tournament," Jan relates, "and I said to my father, 'Oh my gosh. I'm really tired of the traveling. I think maybe I'll just stay home a couple of weeks, and then I can join him.' My dad got so mad at me! He said, 'Absolutely not. You knew exactly what you were getting into. This is your job. You've already been home a week. Your job is traveling with him out there so he's not alone.' And that's all the discussion there was basically. I'm glad he did it, because I was like, 'Well, he's right.'"

For forty-three years Jan has packed up and gone with Peter to his tournaments, cheering him on and being the support he needs, as often as she can. Other commitments may at times pull her away, but for the most part, she's there. But even the time apart has some benefits.

Jan relates, "My son, the smart attorney, did say one time, 'You know, I think it's really good for you and Dad that you get time apart. Then, when you're together, you're always really excited to see each other again.'" Daughter Kristen was once asked what it was like to have a father who was gone so much. She said, "When he's gone, our life just feels normal. When he's home, it's extra special." Jan believes that since she herself didn't resent Peter being gone, she didn't pass that feeling along to the children. She understood why he was gone, and he appreciated what she was doing with the kids at home. After all, he was a golfer from day one of their life together. It was all she and the children ever knew.

Jan tells about one of the more difficult tournaments Peter participated in. The 2004 Senior US Open, Peter's first Senior because he had just turned fifty, tested the couple on many levels. Peter had just withdrawn from the British Senior Open a few weeks prior to the US Open. "He's had so many body parts worked on," Jan says, that she can't remember exactly what it was that made him pull out.

"I don't know how many back surgeries, a shoulder—I mean, every-thing. I think it was a hip. Something was bothering him."

All three of their kids were with them in England for the British Senior Open, and they took advantage of Peter's not playing to take in the sights and do some fun things all together as a family. But Peter was still feeling a bit vulnerable by the time the Senior US Open rolled around. He thought of withdrawing before play started because that would free up the spot for someone else. He knew that once he started, the spot would be gone. But Jan said to him, "Peter, you've earned your spot to be here. Just give it a try."

For one of the few times of his career, Jan pushed him. As she tells it, "I said, 'I really want you to start. I think you need to play.'" (His doctor had confirmed he wouldn't be damaging himself physically.) After the first and second rounds, Peter was leading. Then the third round was rained out, which was a blessing because he really was sore by then. They then had to play two rounds—thirty-six holes—on that Sunday. This was in St. Louis, where it was terribly hot (which might actually have been good for his back). Through all this, Peter kept talking about withdrawing, but Jan wouldn't let him. Jan says, "I'm like, 'Absolutely not.' I just pushed—I don't know why. And he ends up winning the biggest tournament in his career."

In 2013 Peter won the Payne Stewart Award, presented annually to a professional golfer who best exemplifies the values of charac-ter, charity, and sportsmanship. Jan and her family are so proud of Peter's many accomplishments, and receiving this award was extra special because Payne, who passed on in 1999, had been so close to the family.

Peter and Jan are of course avid supporters of a newly-formed charity named after Peter's father: the (Erling) Jacobsen Youth Initia-tive. The organization's website states, "Erling Jacobsen believed that golf, at its core, helps nurture values and build strong character.... Erling felt that golf had become intimidating and even unattainable for beginners and junior players. For those kids, [son] David Jacobsen and the Oregon Golf Association created the Jacobsen Youth Initiative."

Peter's brother David has been the principal engine behind this cause. While not a professional golfer, David was a very strong player and would give lessons to any of the kids who needed some help. He could see that becoming a golfer is sometimes cost-prohibitive for the rising generation, as much as they might love the sport. So, it became his brainchild to do something about it. The Jacobsen Youth Initiative subsidizes the fees for young players, encouraging this next generation of golfers to get to know the sport and to form meaningful relationships with peers and mentors. The organization also runs the annual Erling Jacobsen Tour, which hosts juniors (ages seven to eighteen) to play different golf courses in a fun, stress-free environment without competition. Peter often emcees at the awards dinner for the tournaments.

Ultimately, Jan believes, being a good golfer's wife is the same as being a good spouse in any marriage. It's a lot of the same values—just on steroids because of the stresses of celebrity status, traveling, and everything else. But it's the same decision to commit fully and to put family first. Although it has been a lot of work, and sometimes it's stressful, Jan knows it's all been worth it.

6 Birthday Surprises

What do you give your wonderful golf-loving husband of twelve years for his fortieth birthday? That question had been plaguing my mind for a year and a half, before June of 1997. At least I knew the answer would involve golf.

Lucky for me, I had a part-time job as a sales associate, so I had a small cash flow that I could hide to keep what I came up with a total secret. I also knew I wanted to surprise Steve with something big and unexpected. He is a very devoted father and a great husband. Back then, he never indulged in big expenditures on himself (except for golf). I always appreciated how he made it work out that I could be a stay-at-home mom, which I loved. He deserved a wow birthday.

At that time, we didn't belong to any country club, and Steve wasn't taking lessons on a regular basis. I thought, *How about a golf school and vacation?* After doing some research, I found that *Golf Digest* had a school in Sea Island, Georgia. Happily, the dates coincided with Steve's actual birthday on June 8. I always like celebrating a birthday on the actual date, so it seemed perfect for our daughters and me to go with him. We would just have to leave on the girls' very last day of school that year. I didn't think that would be a big deal until I realized I would have to clean out their school lockers the day before—without them knowing. The details of keeping this a surprise grew by the day.

Steve is hard to surprise anyway, so I was already well-versed in making surprises work. First, you need to tell the fewest number of people possible. Second, you hide cash and any evidence of party planning. Our daughters were ten and eleven, and I knew it would be hard, if not impossible, for them to keep any secret from their dad. So, I didn't tell them anything. I didn't even tell our immediate family. I trusted no one! I did, however, have to ask Steve's boss for the vacation time. He agreed and swore he'd keep my secret.

The plan was put into place. We would all travel to Sea Island the day before the golf school started. Steve would have three full days of lessons and then get to practice his newly-honed skills the following week on several courses in Georgia. The girls and I would enjoy the nice pool. Steve would be elated with this birthday gift, and we'd all have a great time.

In the months of planning, I would take my paychecks to the bank and get cashier's checks to pay for the golf school, book the airline tickets, and pay for the hotel. Since Steve handled paying the bills, I did not want to leave a paper trail. I also asked the hotel and golf school to mail the receipts of confirmation to my neighbor. This almost backfired when the neighbor girl delivered a piece of mail to my husband, but I was able to quickly intercept it.

The week before the trip, Steve was sent out of town on business. That was perfect because I wouldn't have to hide things so much and I could pack. Packing for the girls presented a problem because at their ages they had favorite clothes. If I packed their favorites so they'd have them on the trip, they would be sure to notice the clothes were missing. I decided the easiest thing to do was to shop for some new clothes and pack those. That was fun! I even bought Steve a few new items as well. I was busy from the minute the girls got on the school bus in the morning until the second they returned. Could I really pull this off? I began getting nervous as the date got closer.

The day before the big surprise finally arrived. All of the packing was complete. The girls' things were in one large suitcase, and Steve's and mine were in another. I had thrown in everything I could think of. Ah, the good old days when airlines had no weight limits for luggage—I am sure each suitcase was well over fifty pounds. I put the luggage in the garage with a big blanket over it. Steve's plane from his business trip was getting in late the night before we were supposed to leave. It would be dark in the garage when he got in, and he wouldn't notice a thing.

Emily arrived home from school on the bus, and Laura arrived shortly after. I dropped them both off at a friend's house to play so that I could zoom to their schools and empty their lockers. I was armed with four large shopping bags, two for each. I arrived at Laura's school first and proceeded to work the lock combination. I had casually gotten that out of her a few days earlier. For this surprise, the devil was in the details! I had to think of everything.

I dumped everything into two of the bags and proceeded to the next school. I was worried I might run into some of their friends, but I was lucky and did not. I got Emily's stuff without a hitch and headed for home with all of their books and school supplies. All of the bags got stowed in a dark corner of our basement storage room. I couldn't risk them seeing anything.

I was enjoying a cup of tea to calm my nerves, when all of a sudden I heard the garage door open. Steve was home early! I was shocked; he wasn't supposed to be home until eight that night. The luggage would be staring him in the face in the garage, and all my planning could be ruined in a moment.

I put on a calm demeanor and ran out to the car still outside the garage to greet him. He had finished his meetings and decided to catch an earlier plane home. Thinking quickly during our hug hello, I suggested to him that he take advantage of the nice weather and go to the driving range. I had to get him out of the house, even though he had been gone the whole week! Lucky for me, he loved that idea.

But just before he left, he spotted the luggage lump covered with a blanket in the garage. He said, "What's that?" I simply responded, "Nothing!" He cocked an eyebrow as he drove away. I knew I had to figure out what to do with the luggage.

I sprang into action. Could I hide it under the other car? No, bad idea; it could get run over. What about the basement? No, he would bring his clubs downstairs and see it. The only place I could safely store the luggage would be in the garage attic. I pulled down the narrow staircase and proceeded to haul those fifty-plus-pound suitcases straight up. I thought my arms were going to break. But I managed to get them both up there. After closing up the staircase, I found a large box to throw the blanket over. That way Steve would still think his surprise was under there.

Phew! I was exhausted. I walked into the kitchen to breathe a sigh of relief, and this time needed a beer. I had no sooner sat down to drink it, when Steve walked in again! I asked him to pick up the girls, and I would start dinner. I made something easy while simultaneously doing my usual pre-trip emptying the refrigerator of perishables. That night I could hardly sleep. The anticipation and all the secrecy were totally getting to me.

The morning of the big birthday surprise finally arrived. I woke up at 6:00 a.m. and headed downstairs to make breakfast as usual. Steve was in the shower getting ready for work. The girls were still sleeping and would soon be getting ready for what they thought was their last day of school. I bit my nails grinning.

Steve came down to eat, and the girls joined him. They were excited for their last day and discussing summer plans. I just kept my mouth closed and tried to act normal. I did realize that I would have to stall Steve for about a half hour, because the limo wasn't arriving before he typically left for work. So, earlier, I removed the keys from his car and even hid the spare set. While it caused him to panic and frantically look around the house, this would only work for so long.

I snuck into the other room and called my brother-in-law, asking him to call our house and stall Steve for as long as he could. He didn't know what was going on because I really had kept the secret from anyone who wasn't directly involved in the plans. I simply told him that I was trying to surprise Steve so keep him on the phone for as long as possible.

The limo finally drove up. I sent the astonished girls outside with their big poster. Three days earlier I had told them to make a poster for their dad's fortieth birthday. They knew about the poster, but not about the limo. They had no idea what was going on. I told them to wait outside with the driver—and be ready with the camera!

Steve hung up the phone, shaking his head at my zany brother-in-law, and I told him that I had found the keys in a coat pocket. When he opened the garage door to leave for work, he saw his two girls, the big white limo, and the green neon sign.

We all yelled, "Surprise!"

I said, "Guess what? You're not going to work today!"

He was shocked to say the least.

Everyone helped get the luggage out of the attic, assembly-line style. The last item was Steve's golf clubs. As we were pulling out of the driveway, I told the girls that they weren't going to school, either. We were off to the airport!

We arrived at O'Hare Airport, which was when they found out we were going to Sea Island. Once on the plane, I revealed the rest of the birthday surprise. Steve was going to golf school, and we were all spending ten days at a resort. The smile on his face made all my planning worth it.

It was an awesome vacation. Steve liked the golf instructors and really improved his game. He would come back to the hotel in the late afternoons tired but happy. The girls and I had fun at the pool and the beach. They even liked all of the new clothes that I purchased. We found lots of great restaurants. The best one had an incredible Key lime pie with meringue topping. We ate there twice, just to have the pie.

When I finally revealed all of my secrets in the planning of the trip, Steve was stunned. I still couldn't believe I had pulled it off and kept the secret for so long. Success was achieved, and it created a lasting memory for all of us. Our family time is very important to both Steve and me, as well as time with each other. He's very devoted to the links, but he's devoted to us, too.

Turnabout is fair play, as they say. In January 2007, Steve surprised me with an over-the-top fiftieth birthday—but it didn't turn out quite as he planned. I was headed down to Florida the week before my birthday to get away from Chicago's freezing temperatures and blizzards. Steve planned to join me for some fun in the sun. I told him that if he couldn't get away from work for my birthday—it was really important to me that we be together—I would stay in Chicago. But he assured me that he would be there to celebrate with me. He dropped me off at Midway Airport, kissed me goodbye and said, "See you in a few days."

I was looking forward to walking on the beach and being in our newly-remodeled condo—my little piece of paradise. I arrived at the gate early and started reading a book, oblivious to anything around me. All of a sudden, I heard the familiar voice of my sister-in-law, Jeannie. She was a flight attendant for Delta and made some excuse as to why she was at Chicago's Midway instead of Delta's hub at O'Hare—it sounded logical. Little did I know! Jeannie sat down, and we chatted for a bit. Then she said, "Look at those people over there; they're taking pictures of us!" As my head turned, I spotted with a shock my mother and two of my sisters. They were all coming to Florida with me, compliments of Steve. That sneaky and thoughtful guy had arranged everything.

It had been two years since we had purchased the Florida property. The renovations were just completed, so it was the perfect opportunity to share it with family. The flight was a blast, as we enjoyed cocktails with our free drink coupons. Steve had a rental car all lined up for us, which was confusing to me, since he had bought me a Volvo convertible as an early birthday gift in November. I would soon discover why. At the baggage claim area my other sister Catherine was waiting for us. She had flown in from California. Steve had done an excellent job of orchestrating the entire event and coordinating all of the flights.

With luggage in hand, the six of us headed off to the condo. I couldn't wait to share my piece of paradise with the girls. Steve even called one of my Florida friends to coordinate a few dinners. He thought of everything. We had a fun time, relaxing on the beach in the afternoons and dining at many wonderful restaurants in the evening. (I'm afraid to say, we did not golf.) After four fun-filled days, I dropped everyone off at the airport. Steve was due to come in the next day. I couldn't wait to see him and thank him for a spectacular surprise.

The next day, I drove to the airport ready to pick him up. He called me while I was sitting in the cell phone parking lot to tell me which door he would be coming out of. I pulled up to the door and to my shock, my girlfriend Liz was there! Unbelievable! What was Steve up to now? Happy to see each other, we drove off. I figured that Steve would show up the next day on my birthday, or that he would just pop out of a cake! He knew it was important to me. Who knew what he had up his sleeve?

I awoke with excitement the following morning. My official fiftieth birthday had arrived! I didn't care that I was now a half a century old. The anticipation of seeing my husband was overwhelming to me. Steve was so thoughtful and had planned so many wonderful surprises. I couldn't wait to thank him in person.

Liz and I went out to lunch with another friend, Teri. I kept looking around for Steve to pop out from behind a wall. The expectation and the wait time were killing me. During lunch I received a phone call, saying a delivery had arrived. Could it be Steve? I soon found out it was an edible fruit arrangement from another girlfriend, Krista! The entire day, I kept thinking, *Where are you, Steve?* I called him after lunch, and he told me he would be arriving the next day. Because of all the surprises, I didn't believe him. Surely, he was joking.

That evening, Liz and I drove to downtown Naples for dinner

at Vergina's. We were seated and placed our order. Throughout the entire dinner, I kept thinking Steve would appear. But we had finished the fabulous meal without him. Reality began to set in. Steve was nowhere to be found.

I left the table to retreat to the bathroom for a good cry. Then, I tried to pull myself together as I walked slowly back to the table. I was unprepared for what was waiting for me there — six gorgeous Italian male waiters holding a birthday cake. They began singing, "Happy Birthday." I could hardly hold back the tears — I so wished Steve were there. Liz could see something was up. She thanked the waiters and told them I was traumatized about my age! (I wasn't then, but I would be now. Ha!)

We headed out of the restaurant, and I made a phone call to Steve. He then told me that his flight was scheduled for the next day at 4:30 p.m. I could not comprehend what I was hearing. Steve really wasn't going to be there for my birthday. My heart was crushed. I felt bad for Liz because she knew she wasn't a good substitute for my husband. Sometimes girlfriends can only do so much. (She did make me laugh with a few naughty jokes!)

The next morning, I drove her to the airport. I had apologized for putting a damper on her last evening, but she understood. That day, I cleaned up the condo and still hung on to the disappointment of not seeing Steve on my birthday. When the call finally came from Steve that he was at the airport door #4, I said, "See you soon." I wasn't in the cell phone lot; I was at home. I made him wait and look for me like I had been looking for him for two days. I was still angry.

After forty-five minutes, I finally got to the airport. My first question to him was, "How did it feel to be looking for someone and not have them show up? I did that for two days." He only had to do it for forty-five minutes. At this point, he wasn't sure if he should just get back on the plane.

He had gone to so much trouble to make everything so special and surprise me, but forgot that my one request was for him to be with me. It would have required him to take two extra days off of work, and he decided that the next day would be perfectly fine to celebrate my birthday with me.

I took a deep breath. I asked him if I could vent for ten minutes, and then we could enjoy his visit. He said, "Sure." I got it all out of my system, and he finally understood just how important that detail was. He apologized, we got past the drama, and we had a celebratory dinner the next evening.

I really was glad to see him!

Steve's fiftieth birthday was in June of the same year. I had been researching a trip for him to Scotland, the birthplace of golf, since the year before. I knew he would love to play St. Andrews and many other famous courses there. I had a few things lined up, but then things took a turn from festive to frightening. I discovered a lump in my right breast. After a few tests and a biopsy, I was told I had breast cancer. The wonderful trip to Scotland would have to be postponed. I was to undergo a mastectomy.

The surgeon had an opening on June 8, which was Steve's birthday. I declined and chose June 13. I did not want to remember his birthday that way. We celebrated a very low-key birthday for Steve with dinner out, and I baked him his favorite German chocolate cake. I gave him a book, *Fifty Places to Play Golf Before You Die*, by Chris Santella. It lists the Highlands, the Durness Golf Club, and St. Andrews, the Old Course in Scotland, as numbers forty-three and forty-four. I wrote an IOU note on this page for Steve.

The day before the scheduled surgery, a new prognosis made me decide to have a bilateral mastectomy with immediate reconstruction. It would be good to get it all over with. I had my surgery on June 13 and spent five days in the hospital. Everything went smoothly. The year of reconstruction is now a big blur in my memory. I thank my family, friends, and the Cancer Support Center in Mokena, Illinois, for getting me through the ordeal. It has been twelve years now, and I'm cancer free.

Steve is an excellent golfer, but clearly not a cook. He is capable of flinging a piece of meat on the grill, but he detests cooking. He lives on turkey sandwiches, Milk Duds, and popcorn when I am not around. It's become something of a joke between us.

One time, when he was in Florida and I was stuck in Chicago fulfilling some obligations, he texted me a picture of a beautiful sunset taken from our lanai with the caption, "In case you forgot what it looked like." I had to laugh. I took a picture of our barren backyard, with zero foliage on the barren trees and sent it to him with the same wording. I added, "Maybe you're just missing my good cooking." Then, he told me that he had grilled himself a big steak and made a baked potato. I was impressed that he had used the oven and not the microwave. "You can cook!" I responded. "Maybe when I come into town, you can even cook for me."   ·

The seed was planted, but Steve's culinary skills come out only on birthdays. One year, he made me Belgian waffles from scratch. On another birthday, he even tried baking me a cake.

We had been discussing that if I like to bake so much, why did I always buy a bakery cake for birthday celebrations? "It's all a matter of decorating," I responded. I always want our birthday cakes to look spectacular, and I didn't have the tools, the talent, or the time to do it. It was also a lot easier to check off a bakery cake on the party preparation list. We have a very big family, so it is not unusual to have a party of twenty-five to thirty.

My birthday that year wasn't going to be a big celebration, so who was I to stop Steve's wonderful offer to bake me a cake himself? He looked through several of my cookbooks and came up with two cake choices. One was a German chocolate cake, and the other was a black forest cherry cake. I choose the black forest cherry. Steve headed to the grocery store with his list in hand. Being an efficient man, it took him less than a half hour. I quickly cleared out of the kitchen and relinquished it to him. I decided to do some shopping of my own and headed to the mall.

Several hours later, I returned to find the three layers of the cake on the kitchen counter cooling on the racks. "Hm," I said. "The layers look rather thin," I said. He said that he didn't know why. We reviewed the list of ingredients in the recipe, and he said he had added them all. Not only were the layers thin, but they were curled up at the edges. They looked like rippled Frisbees! I tried hard not to laugh. He had tried. I picked up one of the cooled layers, and it even had a rubbery texture. I think it would have bounced if I dropped it on the floor. *No birthday cake for me this year*, I thought.

Disappointed, Steve threw the layers in the garbage can after I told him it wasn't worth wasting more ingredients to frost them. I did feel bad for him. That evening we were going over to my parents' house with the girls to celebrate. After dinner, I asked if anyone wanted birthday cake. "Sure," they all responded. I then pulled out a white box with the three cake layers that Steve had baked! It was funny, and even Steve was laughing. Over the years, I have realized that I probably shouldn't have done this because he has never attempted to bake me a cake again. As for the mystery of why the black forest cherry cake flopped, sadly it was never solved.

I'm a sentimental person and have saved every card we have given each other over the years. When we downsized from Chicago to be near our grandkids, I decided to recycle the old cards, since there was quite a stash. Our new tradition is to select a card from years past and regive. We both are enjoying some good laughs and fond memories of those special moments. When we are old and our memory is failing, we probably won't notice the difference between a birthday and a Christmas card.

Birthdays are mile markers, and celebrating them with family and friends make them special occasions. Steve and I like to keep it simple. A thoughtful gift, a funny card, and a homemade cake are just perfect for us. We both know that cards and surprises aside, good marriages don't just happen—they take work, commitment, trust, and, most important, love. And thankfully, on those things, we've got a winning team.

7 A Piece of Paradise

I was born in Miami Beach, Florida, and, like the giant loggerhead sea turtles, I have always felt compelled to return there.

I'm passionate about those magnificent creatures. Many hatch on the Florida beaches, and Barefoot Beach is fortunate that many lay their eggs there. Typically, sixty days later the adorable little hatchlings emerge from their eggs. This usually occurs at night so that they don't become a snack for a bird, fish, or dolphin. When they mature twenty-five years later, the females return to where they were born and nest on the same beach.

I can relate. It just took me a little longer to achieve my goal—a second home on the beach. Steve was reluctant about Florida at first, but the idea of playing golf year round lured him in. As for me, once the kids were grown, I just wanted to get out of the freezing Chicago winter weather and bask in the sun.

A business trip of Steve's took us to Marco Island, Florida. For a few days, I ventured off the island and headed into the Naples area. I knew that I wanted to be on Florida's Gulf side—not to be confused with the golf side. I did not want to live on a golf course. I wanted to live as close to the beach as we could afford. I met up with a real estate agent who showed me several properties, but nothing spoke to me. Then I told him about an area that our good friends lived in that I wanted to see—Barefoot Beach. After one visit there, I knew I had found my paradise.

We purchased a condominium in May 2005. It had three bedrooms and two baths and was located directly across the street from the Gulf of Mexico. I couldn't have been more thrilled. As for Steve, several golf courses were within a half-hour drive. He was still working at the time, but our girls were now in college. I could visit fairly often. We decided on the ten-day rule: I could stay a maximum of ten days without Steve. Seven days was never enough for family vacations. With two travel days, you are only left with five full vacation days. But after ten days away, I was always ready to come home. And I missed my husband. The saying rings true, "Absence makes the heart grow fonder." In my infinite wisdom, I figured it would not be good for our marriage if I stayed away longer. To this day, we have rarely broken this rule.

On one of my first solo trips in October 2005, I had just been there about two days when we got the news of a Category 5 hurricane that was due to make landfall off the Gulf of Mexico. Steve told me to leave right away. I attended our neighborhood hurricane meeting that day and left the next. Only one person who attended that meeting, Scott, said that he and his wife, Teri, were staying. They had experienced a few other hurricanes and knew the appropriate measures to take in order to be safe. As for me, I was a total novice. I was sad to leave, but that was the sensible decision. The Naples area did get hit hard, but our beach and our buildings were in good shape after the storm.

I made a lot of friends quickly in the community. I became acquainted with Sandy while walking on the beach one day, and of course it turned out that her husband, Rick, belonged to a beautiful country club called Olde Florida. When she heard how good a golfer Steve was, she said Rick would be happy to take him out for a round. I picked up Steve at the airport that evening and told him I had a little surprise. "Tomorrow, be in the parking lot at nine with your golf clubs, and don't be late!" Rick picked him up in his Porsche, and off they went to Olde Florida.

Steve loved the course and told me all about it over dinner. I think he talked about it for at least three hours nonstop. The course was different than most because it had no signage. The holes weren't numbered. In order to get around, you had to know the course. This would present a major challenge for me. After playing ten holes, I'm so exhausted I don't remember what hole I'm on. I would like to emphasize that it is not physical exhaustion—it is purely mental.

You guessed it. Within three years, we were members of our second club. At this one, Steve is the member, and I am the guest. This means the only day I can play for free in season is the weekly family day on Thursday. Otherwise, I can play with Steve or another member and pay the family guest-rate fee. This is fine with me, since I still have the beautiful beach and our condo, "The Cloud"—a name bestowed upon it by a best friend.

Out of season, May through October, I can play anytime. Then the course is usually so empty that I'm often playing by myself. I run through the full eighteen holes in less than three hours. Playing by myself is kind of therapeutic. I'm more relaxed and enjoy the peacefulness. I'm not antisocial, but sometimes playing by myself lets me enjoy the serenity of the terrain with all its natural beauty.

There are plenty of water holes on Olde Florida, home to many alligators. Whenever I hit close to the water's edge, I survey the pond before going any closer. Once I'm sure there are no alligators near, I quickly hit. If I'm playing by myself, I use a long club to scoop the ball away from the pond. Of course, I know I'm breaking a rule when I don't take the penalty stroke for moving the ball. But then again, I'm playing by myself, so who cares? It makes no sense to risk a gator attack just to hit the ball.

Often you will see golf balls in plain sight near the water's edge that other golfers had to walk away from because of the gators. It's nice to find some free balls, especially because I lose so many. I'm not picky about the brands either. If the ball rolls, I will use it. My husband will only play with Titleist Pro V1 balls. He swears they go farther for him and sometimes give the necessary back spin so they slow down on the green. They are also about four dollars each. That is why I do not play with them. I would rather spend the money on cute golf clothes.

One magical week in the summer, I was in my golfer groove. I played three rounds in less than a week. I shot a repeat of my personal best. The incentive was a margarita at the end of the round. I told myself that if I shot 110 or less, I could have one at the bar. Since it's "the sport of integrity," I waited to order as Mike, the bartender looked at me with quizzical eyes. I never like to add up my score during a round for fear that I could get depressed if it's too high or I could jinx myself if I'm doing well. When I'm in the zone, I like to stay focused and don't want to ruin it. Much to my surprise, I had shot 104! I was so excited; I even double-checked my addition just to be sure. Yes, Margaritaville, here I come!

Now because of that great round, I was sucked in. I realized it was because I had unusually low putts, only thirty for eighteen holes. Steve had taught me to keep track of your shots on the score card; that way you will know where the weakness in your game lies. I was a putting queen that Sunday. Only three days prior, I had needed a navigation system to get my ball into the hole.

That is the nature of the beast. One day you're putting well, but your drives go less than fifty yards. The next time, your drives could be to the moon, but the closer you get to the pin, the farther away the ball wants to go. Every once in a while, though, the stars and the moon align perfectly, and you have a great round with both putting and fairway shots. How is it possible to have a phenomenal score one day and the next day score so poorly it's in the triple digits? God gives some people the talent to play the sport, but it's up to the person to hone their skills. That's why this sport keeps people like me coming back.

When I play by myself, I often play a few balls against one another. My Titleist balls play against Pinnacle, Nike, and Callaway. I don't usually start out that way, but when I hit a shot poorly and know I can do better, I immediately drop a ball and try to replay the shot. Sometimes it does the exact same thing and I'm back to being frustrated, but other times it does exactly what I wanted it to do, and I'm elated. On the score card, I add the new players: Pinnacle, Nike, and Callaway, sometimes complete with the personalities of the famous golfers the brands sponsor. They are now competing with the original Titleist ball that I started with.

This can make for a very long round, especially if I play all eighteen holes that way. It would be the equivalent to playing seventy-two holes of golf. I've never done that for a full round, but I can say my husband has on his unreal male golfer trips. Most often I end up playing forty to fifty holes, especially if the weather is cooperating. I would rather practice on the golf course than the driving range. Playing with four balls is a mental exercise as well. Remembering where they all wind up is a challenge—I've heard mind games help prevent dementia, in which case, I'm doing great.

When playing alone, I have to be my own cheerleader because no one else is there to do it. I may need a pep talk at some point. "Thank goodness, no one saw that last shot, or (worse yet) a whiff!" It is so embarrassing. That's the beauty of playing by yourself. When I strike the ball badly, I almost always know why I didn't hit it well. Steve has drummed it into my skull about looking up too quickly, not turning fully, or using all arms and not my hips to rotate. I know what I'm doing wrong most of the time the instant I do it, so why can't I correct it? That is the million-dollar question. That is why golf pros stay in business. Golfers go back to their old bad habits all the time. It's an endless battle sometimes. I then choose a different weapon in my bag and go after that little white ball. I'm going to continue to battle or die trying.

When the ball flies, you feel elated until it goes into the dreaded sand trap or, heaven forbid, the "Valley of Death." That is the name I gave to hole #11 at Crystal Tree in Orland Park up north. Once you're in it, you're going to die. It is a par-5 hole and has a narrow spot right in the middle that I call the "gauntlet." You have to hit down the hill through a narrow passageway lined with trees, or risk it all and hit over a giant patch of rough grass on your left.

It received the gauntlet name from the 1994 movie starring Kevin Bacon and Meryl Streep, *The River Wild*. In order to stay alive, Meryl Streep has to navigate a raft through a narrow passageway with a Category 6 river rapids rating. This category is so dangerous it can result in serious injury or even death. Works for the golf course, too.

Just when I have recovered from traveling through the gauntlet, the Valley of Death appears. I named this part of the golf hole from the movie *Titanic*, starring Leonardo DiCaprio and Kate Winslet.

As many can recall, the boat is sinking, and passengers on the boat realize they are going to die. It's like walking through the valley of death. The valley at Crystal Tree refers to the enormous swale near the green. It must be fifteen feet deep right near the pin. (Perhaps I'm exaggerating a little.) Once you are in this swale, you are going to have a heck of a time getting the little white ball out of there. Do you putt it out and risk having it roll back into the swale because you did not strike the ball hard enough? Maybe you try to chip it out, but hit it too forcefully and then it ends up on the other side in a sand trap. Golf is not for the timid.

Usually at some point, my internal dialogue with the course creator goes, "What were you thinking, Robert Trent Jones Junior, when you designed this torturous hole? It's a par 5, but it should be an 11. The maximum number of strokes I can take on this hole is eleven, but remember when I took fourteen? Yikes. I'm exhausted just thinking about it. I may need a drink."

Then you move on to the next hole with the intent of doing better, only to find the next hole is a big challenge as well. Just when you're used to teeing off from one spot at the ladies' tees on #12, they move the tee bed to the other side! I recall buying two new clubs for this particular hole just so I could hit it on the green. Spending money on golf goes hand in hand with playing — that's the nature of the game. You must slay the dragon: that's the course. I will stand at the hole thinking, *Which weapon do I choose?* The yardage changed, but the uphill climb is still the same or worse. It's steep with a deep valley in between. *Do I leave the course now and head to the pro shop to buy yet another club? Is this a tricky marketing ploy to get me to spend more money? It is pure genius!*

Having the second home in Florida has allowed us many benefits. Steve and I find it wonderful to play golf year round. When you can only play in the summer, the skills that were acquired get rusty. We are fortunate to have double sets of clubs in both locations; however, certain golf clubs, like Steve's driver and putter, travel with him. They are expensive, and when technology changes, most golfers want to upgrade.

Choosing a second place where your children would like to visit is ideal, especially if you like seeing them. We love our daughters, and they are beach girls like their mother. Steve has a perfect setup with golf and loves not to have to schedule tee times. He just shows up, and the usual "Breakfast Club" starts to play.

As a family, we have bonded over the many activities available in the community we chose. Playing golf, visiting new sights, dining at new local restaurants, walking the beach, biking, and canoeing in the back bay area are adventures that we all still enjoy. We try to keep the activities interesting and fun for all of the participants.

Typically, Steve will join me on the beach about once a week to see the sunset and have a glass of wine. He prefers the sand to be in a sand trap on the golf course, not getting it between his toes, but he shares my time with me when he can. It's such a blessing that we've found our way to our own little piece of paradise.

BUILDING CHARACTER BY GIVING BACK: MANDY SNEDEKER

When people feel blessed and are truly thankful, it's natural to want to share talents or donate to those less fortunate. When I first spoke to Mandy Snedeker, I felt we shared the connection of trying to make a difference no matter how large or small. "Giving back goes hand in hand with success," says Mandy, wife of 2014's Official World Golf Ranking fourth-best golfer in the world, Brandt Snedeker. "You really can't have one without the other. It would be an incomplete circle. You've got to keep the circle moving."

When it came time to choosing a college, Mandy, born and raised in Ohio, wanted one that was strong academically and would also be fun socially. She did not want her alma mater to be too large or too small. Her Chagrin Falls High guidance counselor suggested Vanderbilt in Nashville, Tennessee. Mandy flew down to visit with her dad and loved it.

It proved to be a fateful choice. Mandy's senior-year roommate, Annie, was a communications major and on the golf team. Also a communications major, a fellow golfer named Brandt would often come over and study with Annie. Mandy did not know anything about golf, but Brandt was just a super nice guy. That made an impression on her. "That's one thing that people always ask me," she says now. "They're like, 'Is he really as nice as he seems?' Yes, he is! There's nothing hidden. He's genuine."

Once they started dating, Brandt told Mandy that he wanted to be a professional golfer. She thought, *Sure you do!* "I didn't even know that was a thing," she says. "I had no idea. 'Well,' I said, 'that sounds great. I'm graduating in economics, and I'm going to be an investment banker.'" Mandy's mother and her father, the owner of a successful business, were a little hesitant when she told them she was dating someone who wanted to play golf professionally. Her father told her, "Every guy wants to be in pro sports. But let's be honest—not many can." Mandy did not know how good Brandt was, but she told her parents that she believed in him. "So many dads are into golf, but mine was not," she jokes. "Brandt had to earn his respect the hard way."

Mandy graduated in 2002, a year before Brandt. Like most other econ graduates, she dreamed of a job as an investment banker, so she moved to the nearest big city: Chicago. She shared an apartment in the trendy neighborhood of Lincoln Park with a college girlfriend, but after four months, she could only find a temporary job. She concluded she should move back to Nashville, both to seek employment and to see where her relationship was heading with Brandt.

It turned out to be a wise decision. Mandy secured an account manager position with United Health Care as Brandt finished his final year at Vanderbilt and continued playing amazing golf. As time went on, Mandy pursued her career while Brandt traveled during the week. They both stayed focused on achieving their goals while juggling their peripatetic lifestyle for almost five years.

"We never saw each other. I would fly out Thursday after work and come back early Monday. I was exhausted. It just wasn't feasible for the long term," Mandy says. "It was hard when I first realized that I was going to have to leave my career, and life wasn't necessarily going to be what I thought it was going to be. But I came to terms with that. That was just our relationship."

The travel and being apart wore on them both. Brandt was trying to build his career to the point where he was sure he'd be able to support a wife and family. "He's from the South," Mandy says. "That was very important to him."

Finally, in 2006, Brandt felt the time was right to ask Mandy to quit her job and travel with him everywhere. She told him, "You think I am quitting my awesome job, and we're not even engaged?" In his defense, she found out later, he was already planning to propose. "We ended up getting engaged very shortly after that," she says. "I was like, 'Okay, I'll leave my job now.'"

Brandt proposed that November with a beautiful diamond ring. When it comes to picking out quality stones, Brandt is an expert from having worked in his parents' pawn shop. In fact, his mother had saved a couple of quality diamonds and offered them to Brandt and his older brother when they were only teenagers. Young Brandt had picked the heart-shaped diamond, but when the time came, he decided not to propose with that one. Instead, he turned that diamond into a beautiful necklace for Mandy and gave it to her as a Christmas present a month after their engagement. Because she knows the sentimental story behind the gift, along with the love, Mandy wears this meaningful gift all the time.

In the next two years, Mandy and Brandt traveled internationally for his tournaments to New Zealand, Australia, China, and Japan. It was a great experience to do that as a couple, prior to having children. Mandy is certain one day that she will want to do it all again—maybe without the golf clubs.

"Traveling together like that was really special," Mandy says now. "I'm so glad we did it. We went everywhere. Our honeymoon was in New Zealand while he was playing a tournament, then on to Fiji. China, Japan—I mean, we got to do all that. And that's one thing I tell younger women out on tour. You're going to get married. You're going to have kids. So I say, 'Don't rush it.' I think that a lot of them feel pressured to get married and have the kids, but I'm here to say just enjoy it. You have all these opportunities to travel with the guys everywhere."

In the golf world, even if you're making big purses, you still have to be able to manage the money intelligently. For Mandy and Brandt, it always made financial sense to live within their means and keep a cushion. "I think with athletes in general, it would shock you how much money they make," Mandy explains. "But many actually don't have as much money as you would think because they blow it. Brandt has been very successful, but once you're on the Champions Tour, you don't get the same sponsorship money. I mean, we're very blessed. But you want to be smart. If something were to happen, an injury where he couldn't play or he doesn't play as well or you name it, whatever, that's an extra stressor. We already have enough going on—that's the last thing he and I wanted to worry about. So we're pretty conservative when it comes to that kind of stuff.

"Our relationship is probably atypical in that I'm the one who handles more of the finances and bills. It's probably not normally the case, but that's the personality I have. He's very laid back. That's what makes him so good. He just doesn't like to have to think about a lot of things. He can clear his mind very easily, whereas I'm very type A. That's always been the way we are. Ever since we were engaged and started making a life together, that's been my role.

"We have been together since college. So we have gone

through the whole process together—through the college career, the amateur career, all the way till he turned pro," Mandy says. "I always joke that life in general is obviously up and down, but golf is like a roller coaster. That applies to everybody; doesn't matter how good you are. I mean, Tiger Woods, Phil Mickelson—they all have ups and downs. When you play for that many days in a row, you cannot be good every single day. It's not like other sports."

The couple married in 2008, seven years into their relationship. On October 18 that year, Mandy and Brandt took vows in a lovely garden ceremony at the Cheekwood Botanical Gardens in Nashville. Her sister, Sarah, was the maid of honor and Brandt's brother, Haymes, was his best man. The reception was in the old stable and courtyard next to Cheekwood Mansion. Family friend and country music legend Vince Gill sang "When Love Finds You" for their first dance—quite a surprise for their wedding guests.

Then it was life on the road again for a few more years—until they started their next adventure: children.

Brandt almost missed the birth of their first child in 2011. "I went into labor two weeks early with Lily, my first," Mandy says. "Brandt was actually in Florida." He had a tournament down there, and the baby was not due for two weeks. "The doctor said I was fine, and he left."

Brandt had an early tee time the next morning—right about when Mandy started to feel something. Still, she did not want to admit to herself what was happening.

She laughs when she remembers thinking, *Hmmm, is this labor?* "Looking back, I should have called Brandt, but I didn't know if it was real or not." She decided to wait to call him until after he finished his round.

Once he was done, Mandy finally made that call. By then she

knew it was for real, and that it was progressing rapidly. Brandt raced to the airport, but there were no direct flights to Nashville. In the meantime, Mandy went to the hospital with her mother and a good friend while she waited for either Brandt or the new baby to make an appearance first.

Just minutes before Mandy was about to deliver, the anxious father-to-be sprinted down the hospital hallway—an important competition to win! Brandt made it just in time to witness the birth of their little girl, Lily.

Their second child was due in early October 2012, which would have been perfect for the typical golf season. But that year Brandt was scheduled for both the FedEx Cup in late August and the Ryder Cup in late September. Mandy especially did not want to miss the Ryder Cup, which took place up near Chicago. She opted to stay home in Nashville and miss the FedEx Cup Tour Championship in Atlanta the week before. Of course, when Brandt won in Atlanta, it hurt that she was not there to witness that big achievement.

"I was not at the FedEx Cup when he won because I was literally two weeks out from having our son. I knew I couldn't do both. I mean, I was very pregnant. It was Brandt's first Ryder Cup team, so I was like, 'I am not missing this.' And it was near Chicago. I thought, 'Oh, they've got great hospitals if I go into labor.' So I didn't go [to the FedEx Cup]. I didn't know he was going to win!" Brandt ended up winning on the fourth day of play.

Mandy was now thirty-eight weeks pregnant. She flew with Brandt to be by his side for the Ryder Cup at Medinah Country Club outside Chicago. "Basically," she says, "I almost went into labor Sunday night after all that time on my feet." She started having contractions, so they did not even make it to the closing ceremonies. Luckily, the contractions subsided, and she was able to make it home to Nashville. Their healthy baby boy, Austin, made his entrance a few days later.

Now, with children, Mandy and Brandt's life as a couple and a family went in a genuinely new direction. "Before," Mandy says, "we lived and died by golf. It's just what we did. I traveled everywhere with him. I watched every single hole. It was our entire life. And then we had children. It changed everything—I think for the better. Especially for Brandt. He was consumed by golf because it just requires so much mental focus. I think when we had our daughter, it made him look at everything. Obviously, everybody knows this—when you have kids you just look at life differently."

The couple made the decision to travel as much as possible as a family while the kids were tiny—but this commitment was not without its challenges. For a while after Austin was born, so close in age to Lily, Mandy and Brandt wondered, "What did we do to ourselves?" But they quickly grew to love having their two little ones with them on the road. Hiring a nanny when Austin was born to travel with them really helped. Another huge benefit was that the tour offered a traveling daycare. This gave the children consistency, since they had regular care providers they could get to know. Many of the other tour families had children in the same age bracket. When they were all in a new city, the moms would take the kids to the local zoo, to a playground, to lunch, and out for ice cream. "We all tried so hard to keep some kind of normal for our children," Mandy says.

One special family event takes place in Augusta, Georgia, at the Masters every year. On Wednesday at the par-3 course, the children get to caddie for their fathers. The participating kids are clothed in the signature white coveralls, complete with the player's name on the back. They get their pictures taken and walk around the course. This was always a big highlight for both Mandy and Brandt.

As parents, Mandy and Brandt have found that building character in a child who has everything is a constant concern. "We talk about that all the time," she says. "Of course, it's not their fault that they have everything, but you want to make sure that they know that they're blessed and that it's not necessarily guaranteed for them. They should always have a heart of giving. One good thing I would say with them being older now is that we can lead by example. If they see you out there serving the community, that's going to become something that they think that their family does." The couple has made giving back a family priority.

Even before she and Brandt were married, Mandy joined the Junior League (a national women's organization that promotes volunteerism, develops member potential, and improves communities through the action and leadership of trained volunteers) in Nashville. "The Junior League matches you with a nonprofit in town," Mandy explains, "and I got set up with Our Kids."

Our Kids is a nonprofit dedicated to increasing community awareness of child sexual abuse, providing expert medical evaluations and crisis counseling since 1987. The organization also offers education and training about the issue.

Before her involvement, Mandy had no idea that an organization for sexually abused children existed in Nashville. "They cannot market the kids on posters because it is so awful and a traumatic experience in itself," Mandy says, "but the word must get out that there is a need." National statistics reveal that one in ten children will go through some form of sexual abuse by age eighteen, not to mention the unknown numbers of cases that are never reported. These children are in desperate need of medical evaluation and crisis counseling. The Our Kids mission touched Mandy's heart, and she continues her commitment to making a difference.

One of her first projects with them was to spearhead the creation of a colorful, informative flyer that gave clear instructions about how to talk about abuse with young children. "It's very simple things that I never would have thought twice about," Mandy explains. "For instance, the social workers there would say that if a child opens up to you about a possible sexual abuse claim, your instinct might be to say, 'Hey, it's okay; you can tell me—I won't tell anybody.' Well, if they are being sexually abused, they already have somebody telling them that. If you then go on to tell somebody, with all good intentions, the child just sees that as another person they can't trust."

Kids are very literal. Another tip on the flyer is that you shouldn't say, "Don't let anybody touch you." This may make a child feel like they did something wrong if they "let" it happen.

It's also good to avoid making a joke out of secrets themselves. "A lot of parents say, 'Let's have a secret,' and we think that's cute and funny. But also, we have to make it very clear that there are secrets that are fun and appropriate with Mommy and Daddy, but if somebody ever tried to tell you not to tell us because they're touching you, that's not a good secret. We just need to have very open conversations.

"I'm a mother with young kids," Mandy says. "It makes sense that not everyone would know these things. To us at Our Kids—because we work with these kids and talk to them—we know how the predators work. Sadly, it is such an issue. It's always been an issue. As you can tell with all these national stories, this has been happening for a long time.

"Unfortunately, a very high percentage of predators are somebody that the child knows." It's not usually some stranger who tries to get the child to do something. "The kids would be like, 'Of course, I'm not going to do that.' When it's somebody they trust, they're going to listen. The person will take advantage of that child. It's scary to think about. But I think it's really important to get the word out there and talk about it. Even within Nashville, there are so many people who come to us and say, 'That happened to me, and I didn't have anywhere to go.' It's been really powerful in the past ten years being with them."

In addition to Our Kids, Mandy and Brandt always had a dream to have their own foundation. Brandt had strong years on the tour in 2012 and 2013, and he and Mandy had had their children by then. "We both have given back to the community, and I've been on the board at Our Kids," Mandy says, "but we thought it'd be really cool to do a foundation, too. We didn't know when the timing would be right. After 2013, the timing seemed right, both financially and with his name recognition."

They decided to use Brandt's growing fame to become a sponsor of a junior golf tour. After much planning and organizing, they launched their foundation in January 2015. Initially, it was hard to move as quickly as Mandy wanted, but since fall of 2017, when both their kids were in school, she's been able to devote more time to it.

The Snedeker Foundation has raised more than $1 million for several different charities across Tennessee, including Our Kids. Brandt also wanted to give children more of an opportunity to play golf, so they worked with the Tennessee Golf Foundation to revitalize their junior golf program. The result is the Sneds Tour, which sponsors a year-round junior golf tour aimed at allowing kids to learn, play, and enjoy the game of golf while also making competition more affordable through lower entry and registration fees.

Brandt leveraged his becoming more and more well known to build a significant online platform, which contributes to his ability to give back by promoting causes he and Mandy care about. "Brandt has a team, and I'm part of it," Mandy says. "People we know in the community and through golf are on our board at the foundation. Putting that all together and using those resources and those skills is making it as successful as it can be. Brandt is from Nashville; he grew up here. So he's got a lot of roots here."

The foundation also teamed up with the Nashville Sports Council to award four college scholarships annually. "They were more than happy to have Brandt come on," Mandy says. "He wants to make sure that even when his name is not as 'out there' and he's not at his peak, that doesn't mean the kids are going to suffer. We want to try to build an endowment, so that it's always there.

"To be able to do that feels really good. I think Brandt and I both forget sometimes that we live in our own world. Like, I've known him forever. My children, too—that's all they know, that's their father. They don't think twice about his success. But the power he has when we see him with the junior golfers, when he gives talks to them or when he shows up at a tournament, how excited they are, how they listen—that's impactful. It's cool to see."

When asked, "If your husband was a golf club, which would he be?" Mandy responds, "I guess it would be a driver. I feel like I am constantly behind and never getting anything done. Maybe he would be able to help me get further and faster." Brandt will come home and ask, "What did you do today?" Mandy's response is often, "I don't know! I can't tell you—I was so busy!"

Mandy's days are full with two children, the foundation, and Our Kids. "I'm still very active with Our Kids," she says. "That's my passion; junior golf is Brandt's. So we're fifty-fifty." Whenever she finds that spare moment, she tries to get in a workout.

Life with a golf pro presents some challenges as well. The most challenging times for Mandy have been when Brandt was injured and unable to play. "He doesn't know what to do with himself," she says. "He's crawling the walls." And Brandt has had his fair share of injuries. "There have been several where he's had to take months off and didn't know how long it was going to be before he could play again. That was challenging in that we just had to trust. Not being able to do what you love is not a financial thing at that point." Mandy adds, "I would say a lot of guys out there don't love golf. They have been blessed with the talent, and it's very much a job to them. But Brandt loves golf. He loves practicing, he loves playing. He always has, ever since he was a little kid. So seeing him not be able to do that and have the worry of maybe he won't be able to do it—that has been really challenging."

One of their best times was Brandt's win at Wyndham in 2018— and of course, it's because of their kids. "Our kids had been there before when he won," Mandy says, "but they were so young. They don't really remember it. So this was the first time he won where the kids [ages seven and six] were so excited. They were so nervous on the eighteenth green and couldn't wait to run out and tackle him when he won. Just seeing them so proud of their dad and so excited for him . . . he would probably say the same thing. That is probably one of our best memories."

"Celebrations are a must in the ups and downs of the game," Mandy says. She and Brandt typically celebrate after a good round with dinner out and a bottle of wine. Sometimes she gets a group of friends together to have a little celebratory party. If he loses, it is just part of the deal. "The guys are so good, they are not really happy unless they are winning and not satisfied with anything less. They know they possess the skills to do it but realize that they cannot win all the time." For Mandy, this has been a learning experience. She and Brandt are in this together. One year, you can be "Player of the Year" and "The FedEx Champ." Then, the next year, you're sure you'll get even better and maybe you don't. Mandy and Brandt have worked through these times as a couple.

Another great element to being on the tour is all the fantastic friends they've made—all across the age spectrum. "That's the funny thing about golf," Mandy says, laughing. "They just keep getting younger and younger. Brandt has been out there for twelve years now. We're kind of like the grandparents. We're friends because we all have that one common denominator. Golf is such a different life that it's hard for other people to understand. It's such a leisurely thing for a lot of people, including CEOs, other athletes, and musicians—other people who are very successful at what they do. But for Brandt and our friends on the tour, it's their job. With that common denominator, it doesn't matter whether you're twenty-two and single, twenty-five and engaged, or longtime married with grandchildren. You can put us all in a room, and everybody gets along.

"I think that Brandt is a good example of how quickly they mature. They start so young doing what they're doing, often right out of college. That kind of forces them to be at a level of maturity that most people probably aren't at at that age. It can work, or it can backfire. Some of our dearest friends are so much younger than us, but so mature for their age. We have all gone through that process. They are doing things we did five years ago. And there were older people who were mentors to us in the same way. They're all great friendships."

So what does the future hold for Mandy and Brandt? Mandy doesn't know what it will look like exactly, but she's sure it will involve continuing to grow their foundation and being active in the community.

"Our house is immersed in serving and giving back," Mandy

says. "It's nice for the kids to see that. Now that they're a little bit older—almost seven and nine—the past year has probably been the first time they started asking about it. 'What do you do? How does it work?' Those are really good conversations to have."

8 Retired, Not Retired

Good conversations to have especially with your spouse include the subject of retirement. It came somewhat as a surprise to me that Steve decided to retire from BMW Constructors Incorporated at the young age of fifty-three in 2011. He had worked very hard at this industrial construction company for the prior twenty-three years and held the position of vice president of construction for the last twelve. Now, I wondered, what would it be like to have him home more often?

I remembered the time my friend Liz and I were baking an apple pie for Steve while he was watching a golf tournament on TV. We wanted to ask him something, but I told her it would have to wait until the commercial. Then I told her the way to my man's heart is through his stomach and letting him enjoy his hobby. Would this work even in retirement?

True golfers want to play golf all the time, watch it on TV if they are not on the course, and can talk hours on the subject. When they can't do any of those things, they are thinking about golf. It truly is a cultlike existence. You get to know more people who play the sport, and soon you're booked for the entire week. That is my husband's job now. He plays golf five or six days a week, depending on the weather.

To ease my worries, Steve brought me a book by Dave D'Antoni, one of his golf buddies, called *The Globe-Trotting Golfer's Guide to Retirement*. The book talks about planning ahead for retirement, how to get along with your spouse when you are home more often, and golf trips and travel. No thinking required; I just read this book. It took me three days and calmed me down considerably.

When Steve read the book, it simply confirmed that he had done one of the most important things, which was to purchase your home for your retirement years before you actually retire. By doing it that way, you become comfortable with the expenses and know you can afford it. He also had his hobby, golf, to occupy most of his free time.

The travel part does include me on most of our vacations. Scattered in the year are one or two male-bonding golf trips. We are now doing a lot of traveling, and we can get great deals since we can go anytime. We have nothing else to do, right? Well, this is not totally true, with a growing number of grandchildren, my volunteer job, cooking, cleaning, and maintaining two properties. The properties are smaller, but there is always something to do.

I think this has worked well for us. It took some hard learning on my part to understand what goes on in Steve's brain and to understand the passion he feels for golf. Several months after he retired, I came to the realization that the routine he had developed would not change on a day-to-day basis. It was up to me to adjust to this and go with the flow. However, if there were something that directly affected me in a negative way, I would speak my piece.

Thankfully, there was never anything major, and Steve is good at compromising. In retirement, you do not have to be together every waking moment. Time apart is better for conversations later.

I love to bike and rollerblade, but I don't want to do it every day of the week. A variety of activities is much more fun for me. I'm all for adventure and trying new things, like paddleboarding with my friend Cheryl. The back bay waters provided the peaceful environment—until I found out there were gators back there. The Gulf of Mexico can be a challenge, especially if there are waves, but that is a safer environment.

It's not that Steve won't do other things besides golf. We love movies. Steve isn't a big boater, but he will go with me. We bike together and walk on the beach, although sometimes it turns into a run, and he leaves me in his sand dust. Dining out at wonderful restaurants with friends or ourselves is marvelous. Although Steve's scale is tipped toward golf, there is a balance.

According to our financial planner, the first couple of years of retirement are critical, so he warned us not to go over budget. But then, our youngest daughter, Emily, announced she had decided to get married. This took us by surprise, but we were thrilled for her and loved the guy. "Don't go over budget" are wise words, but how could we deny our girl anything? Both girls are so wonderful, and we were so elated about the event.

Weddings, however, require money. We had a pretty good idea of the cost because our oldest daughter, Laura, married Brad two years earlier, with a fancy downtown Chicago wedding. Thank goodness, Steve was still employed then. Emily and Ben, on the other hand, loved the outdoors, so they chose the Morton Arboretum in Lisle, Illinois—a breathtaking, beautiful place to have the ceremony and reception. As some of the wedding details were being checked off the list, Laura and Brad announced that they were expecting their first child. The baby was due one month before the wedding. With so many exciting things happening, our travel plans went on the back burner.

Exactly a year before retiring, we upgraded our Florida abode to a slightly larger condo with better views. The property is located directly next door, in the same complex. I think being there is like a vacation because we are constantly on the go with our friends, neighbors, and house guests. Eating out is the best, as there is an abundance of amazing restaurants with delicious cuisine.

As much as I enjoy eating out, I do like to cook. Sometimes I wish it were an activity that Steve and I could do together. Having a glass of wine while making something deliciously creative would be my idea of a nice quiet evening. Maybe Steve is still scarred from the birthday cake fiasco.

His retirement, which made him available for housework, prompted our new deal: I cook and he cleans. I admit I was guilty of purposely dirtying extra bowls, pots, and pans to see if he would ever switch jobs, but he never caved. As it stands now, I'm the head chef, and he is the dishwasher. He is speedy and efficient. Since he has taken up this job, we have had only a few broken glasses, a few chipped dishes, and one broken serving platter. At least with this plan, I'm partly retired, too.

We have now gotten into the retirement groove. I get up early and fix breakfast. Steve makes the bed (in our household, the last one out makes it). Steve likes to eat breakfast with me and read the paper. He then does the dishes and heads out to the course to join his friends in the Breakfast Club, where he gets a second helping of that most important meal of the day. The Breakfast Club then goes out to play eighteen holes of golf. Although there is some friendly wagering, retired men usually don't like to bet big—that's a good thing. Steve also eats lunch at the club, so that's one less meal I have to prepare.

This routine is very typical for five or six days a week. I enjoy the peace and quiet once he is gone. When the TV is on (which it is when he is home), I accomplish nothing. During basketball season, all I can hear is the noise of squeaky shoes on the court—like nails on a chalkboard. I'm thankful that I created a man cave in the condo with almost soundproof doors. If I hadn't done that, happily married might not have survived happily retired!

Retirement requires compromises, respect, and leaving the remote control alone when we are watching TV. What is it with men and TV remotes? It practically becomes part of their anatomy. Maybe Steve is slightly more skilled at fast-forwarding through commercials, but does that really matter if a few seconds get shaved off? We DVR a lot of programs to save time. I'm even okay with watching golf tournaments, although I must confess, I go in and out of a room because I can't sit still that long. You might be surprised to know that Steve is a willing partner to watching *Dancing with the Stars* and *The Bachelor*. In my defense, we also watch *The Rookie*, *America's Got Talent*, and the news. There would be more blood-and-guts TV shows, but out of respect for me, they are never on when I am around.

When it comes time to watching the Master's Golf Tournament, though, Steve is glued to the set and only leaves to use the facilities. I think if there were a tree near the TV, he would use it, which brings to mind a significant fact about golf—men seem to go everywhere on the golf course. Women have a much harder time, which is why for years I begged my husband, who was on the house committee at Crystal Tree, to get another bathroom on the course. They finally settled on two deluxe porta-potties. I'm thankful. It's better than the bushes!

The other benefit of my husband retiring is I get free golf lessons—from him. Steve is a busy man for being retired. It didn't take me long to realize that if my golf lessons with him weren't scheduled, they would not happen. Wednesday became the lesson day, since we are both at the club for yoga. When Steve heard it could improve his core strength and flexibility for his golf game, he was on board. This past Christmas I purchased him a T-shirt that says, "Real Men Do Yoga." The club instructor, Kathy, is wonderful, and we have both noticed an improvement in our golf games.

After Wednesday morning yoga, the two of us hit the driving range with a passion. Our bodies are all warmed up and loose. Mine is as relaxed as I can get, since I'm a fairly tight person and carry rocks of tension in my shoulders. I'm working on it by stretching a little more and not dwelling on each shot. When I get ready to swing, I say to myself, "Golf is a lazy game—swing nice and easy." Now I do realize that golf is not a lazy game, but for me I have to try hard not to swing with all arms. When you swing relaxed and with a good, even tempo, the ball goes where you want it to in most cases. That's what my beloved personal instructor has told me many times.

When the two of us get out on the range for my lesson, two things always happen. First, Steve decides he wants to work on his own swing and inevitably picks up one of his clubs and starts hitting. I have to remind him, "This is my time! My previous professional instructors didn't do that, and you, my dear husband, shouldn't either." He then puts down his club and starts to pay attention to my swing. But when I am swinging poorly with a club, especially a new one, he wants me to know just how powerful it is. He takes the club out of my hands and then proceeds to hit the little white ball into the next town. "See what that club can do?" he says with a big grin. I quickly take the magic club away from him and try to emulate as best as I can.

The second thing that happens during my lesson is that someone else (you know who you are) will come up to Steve and ask for help. I have to bite my tongue not to say, "Hey, this is my lesson. I married the guy. I cook, I clean, and I do his laundry. Back off." It maybe doesn't come out of my mouth, but it does go through my brain. Polite Steve goes over to assist and comes back eventually.

The worst thing he can say to me is, "So-and-so has a natural swing." I think to myself, *What the heck is mine?* Unnatural of course, but I try not to feel bad because in my head I know there is nothing natural about the sport, except maybe the walking from the cart to hit the ball. Walking I will admit is natural.

In spite of these foibles, Steve is an amazing coach. The official lesson usually lasts an hour to an hour and a half. By the end, I am almost always hitting crisper shots in the direction I want. My putting and chipping have improved dramatically. It is also fun having little contests on the practice range. I used to think I wasn't competitive, but with Steve I find it totally fun.

Our lesson is usually finished in time for Steve to play the noon game with his pals. At that point, he's ready for some real competition.

Everyday living is definitely different when a husband, wife or both become retired. Our experience was no exception, with changes and compromises being made frequently. Sometimes in golf you have to be a team player by encouraging, helping each other, and understanding that often the perfect shot may land in an unrepaired divot. Learning how to get out of this tough spot is the key. The same strategy works for surviving retirement.

Retirement is like a round of golf. You plan your shots, work with your teammate, and hopefully you get better each round. If not, you plan some more and learn not to bet big. If communication, enjoyment, and affection are always improving, you know you're on the way to the Masters.

9 Living Like a Celebrity

The opportunity to play golf so often once he retired made it easy for Steve to up his game. His handicap dropped to that all-time low of zero, so he was seriously ready to kick some patootie. When the club championship came along, the stakes were high—bragging rights for an entire year.

After making it to the final round of the championship, Steve should have had it in the bag. However, of course, there had to be that one person left who could give Steve a run for his money.

Lou had a phenomenal short game, which means he could chip and putt with amazing accuracy. He had a two handicap and had shot his current age of seventy-five or less 192 times over the years. For any nongolfers out there, that is simply amazing.

The final round of the championship took place on March 17. Steve and Lou started playing at 8:10 a.m. Earlier that morning, I woke up at 5:45 to prepare my hero the breakfast of champions: a glass of juice, a steaming bowl of oatmeal with some brown sugar on top, and a slice of homemade banana bread. Carbs are the name of the game. Steve would top it off with a large cup of coffee once he arrived at the club.

I drove over separately at 9:10 to watch the back nine holes. The scenery zipped by very fast as I gripped the wheel. Whoa, the speedometer was twenty miles over the speed limit! I hadn't even realized that I was speeding. I was nervous for Steve and anxious to see him. It was one of those times I felt I could channel what being a pro golfer's wife must be like.

I arrived at the perfect moment. Steve was just coming off of hole #9 and ready to do the next nine. However, he was down two holes. This was match play, so you don't officially count a score; you just try to beat your opponent's score on each hole. On the front nine, they only tied on one hole; all of the other holes Steve was either winning or losing. It was now five to three in Lou's favor, with one tie. Steve had a big challenge ahead of him.

On hole #11, a par 3, I thought for sure Steve would win it. Lou hit his ball into the sand trap, and Steve was on the green with only a five-foot putt. However, Lou blasted his ball out of the trap, and it landed right in the cup! We all applauded—it was a fantastic shot. Lucky for Steve, he sunk his putt for a tie.

The game went on like that, with both of the men making phenomenal shots to tie each hole. Finally, Steve won hole #13. Now he was only down one hole. On #18, he made his putt to win the hole. The men were officially tied. Time for the sudden death playoff starting back at hole #1.

I was biting my nails by this point along with the rest of the crowd—all nine of us. Okay, maybe it wasn't the same as the hundreds of people surrounding the greens and fairways in professional games. But I still felt the pressure!

Hole #1 of Sudden Death was a par 4 with water on the right and sand traps and trees on the left. Both men had decent drives. Steve could outdrive Lou by twenty to thirty yards, due to the age factor.

But Steve's second shot came up short!

Then Lou's shot did as well!

Steve then took the safer side of lagging his third shot up to get closer to the hole.

Lou's third shot went over the green, leaving him with a very long final putt.

Steve two-putted for a bogey. He was done, with five shots for the hole.

Lou then putted his ball down to the pin. Then—he missed his second putt! The crowds were going wild! He made his third putt for a double bogey on that final hole, but it was too late. Steve was the winner!

(Nail-biters make for excited play-by-plays, don't they? I'm starting to sound like Steve!)

I ran toward Steve to kiss him congratulations. I was so thankful that it was over; my stomach had been in a knot the entire time. Being the wife on the sidelines can be very stressful. You want your husband to play his best, but golf is not easy, and mistakes are made. That is the nature of the game.

We joined Lou, his wife, and her sister at the for a drink and to have some lunch. At first, we joked about them not wanting to sit with us, but then we found a table together and laughed and talked about the round. Steve was awarded a trophy, and we did the photo shoot. And I would now reign for an entire year as the proud wife of the husband who won the Olde Florida's 2013 Club Championship.

The week that followed the championship was great for Steve, when the "celebrity" life really kicked in. I always consider it my wifely duty to tell our family and friends about Steve's successes on the golf course. That way they can congratulate him, and it doesn't make it look like he's bragging. Steve's ego is never out of whack (unless he's around me). I really went the extra mile to fulfill my duty this time. I was so proud!

Steve received lots of congratulatory text messages about winning the championship, but a little later, something even more astonishing happened. One of his friends was watching the PGA tournament and saw Steve in a Titleist golf ball commercial. Steve was famous! Ha, not really. In October 2012, Titleist had asked to film a club fitting Steve was having with the head pro at Olde Florida, in which the pro calculated Steve's golf swing to find the perfect clubs for him. Steve said, "Sure!"—what else is a retired guy to do? The pay was a pair of golf shoes. (The other guy being filmed negotiated a better deal; he received shoes, a hat, and a shirt.) Neither of them thought they would use the footage for television.

Then, a few days after his starring role in the Titleist commercial, Steve got the best gift of all: he made a hole in one on hole #5 at Olde Florida. It was the second of his life; the other happened in his college years. I think he was more thrilled with that second hole in one than with anything else.

I was out of town, helping to host a baby shower for our older daughter, so Steve sent me a picture of the poster the clubhouse had made to commemorate his achievement. He celebrated with an Arnold Palmer. We joked that if he had made it at Crystal Tree, he would have gotten a nice chunk of change because they have a "Hole in One Club." All of the members there put in ten dollars, which you then collect when you get one. He had to settle for bragging rights at Olde Florida.

Steve had an amazing month with winning the championship, the Titleist golf commercial, and a hole in one. As for me, I got to bask in the brighter-than-usual limelight of being the proud wife. We were both stars. If only for a short time, these moments create joyous, lasting memories for both of us. He is doing what he loves for as long as he can. Who knows what will happen next?

NORMAL PEOPLE, GOOD AT SOMETHING: STACY HOFFMAN

For some people, being in the limelight isn't important. They would rather remain incognito, as is the case with Stacy Hoffman. She prefers not to wear her badge and instead likes to be a regular spectator in the crowd, interacting among the people while watching her husband, pro golfer Charley Hoffman.

Stacy grew up in Poway, a small town north of San Diego, California, with an older brother and younger sister. Their parents provided a nurturing environment that encouraged the kids to do anything and everything when growing up, as long as they had an interest. The adventures were numerous and boatloads of fun. When they tried new things, their parents were their cheerleaders. Ironically, none of the children ever played golf.

At Poway High School, Stacy loved all of the activities and was class president both junior and senior year. She played on the basketball team her freshman year, and was on the swim team for a year. Those years truly flew by with being on the social committee to plan the events, committing to academics, and playing team sports. Her parents always stressed the value of a good education and encouraged hard work to achieve a goal. They felt that opportunities would open up if the children had a good education.

And yes, Stacy didn't have to go far to meet her eventual husband. Though they met when they were younger, she got to know him better at Poway High. Charley's focuses in high school, besides the education, were golf and soccer. Having an early start at the age of seven certainly helped. Charley won the California state high school golf championship in 1994 and 1995, becoming the first two-time winner. He and Stacy had so many friends in common that they would run into each other frequently. Some of Stacy's closest girlfriends had even been in Charley's kindergarten class.

When Stacy was home from Boston University and Charley from the University of Nevada, Las Vegas, they both went with a group of their mutual friends to the river to camp. The boating and jet skiing were a total blast, and the embers between them started to spark. Even with all this path-crossing, the dating didn't officially start until after college.

Their first date was going to the movie *The Sixth Sense* with Haley Joel Osment and Bruce Willis, with the famous line, "I see dead people." It was a scary movie for a first date, but that did not matter. Stacy recalls the bigger deal was they both had new cars, and Charley insisted on driving, even though his blue Blazer was in the shop. Stacy was proud of her new black 1999 Jetta that she bought with her own money, but Charley picked her up in his rental car that evening, even though she had offered to drive.

Many of their beginning dates were group dates because of their mutual friends. They saw each other on all of their school breaks and both graduated in 1999. Stacy's degree was in public relations, so she worked for a PR firm in New York City. Charley had turned pro in 2000 and was living in Las Vegas playing mini tours. When he had a break, he would visit her in New York and stay with one of his roommates from college. On Christmas Day when Stacy was home for the holiday, the two would join her family to play board games. One year, when a friend of theirs from New York arrived, dancing and laughing took over. Stacy had a blast.

The proposal came in 2007 during the Callaway Invitational at Pebble Beach, which takes place in November. This pro-am event is very casual, as the amateurs are not too serious as players—most of them like to party and consume wine.

After the golf round, Charley took a short nap, woke up, and suggested going to the beach to build a fire. Stacy thought that was strange because there was a large fire pit at the hotel, but she didn't say anything. Sure enough, after they lugged some firewood and a fine bottle of wine down to the beach, Charley started the fire, filled their glasses, and then got down on one knee to propose. Charley said, "I'm not sure the ring is going to fit!" Her response? "Oh, it'll fit." After their six-plus years of dating, Stacy would make it fit.

On the way to dinner with a friend visiting from San Francisco, Charley said, "Don't tell him and see if he notices." It was so hard for Stacy not to blurt out her excitement. Lucky for them, he noticed the ring by the time dessert arrived. Charley had picked the ring out all by himself, and he did a great job, although Stacy says now, "I didn't care about the ring; all I wanted to do was take the next step and be with him."

A year later, Stacy and Charley were married on November 29, 2008. The large wedding with 220 guests took place over Thanksgiving weekend. Finding just the right venue for the reception was important to Stacy. She wanted that intimate feeling, and she found that at Estancia La Jolla Hotel. It would be perfect because everyone who would stay at the hotel was either family or friends. But once that decision was settled, the wedding planning took an interesting turn.

Charley happened to joke that he wanted to wear a powder-blue tuxedo. At first, Stacy thought, *No way!* But she changed her mind when she realized that she was getting to wear what she wanted, and so should Charley. They googled powder-blue tuxedos, and the movie *Dumb and Dumber* came up. They both started laughing and said, "We should do this!" Stacy and Charley figured it would be a fun prank for the reception, so they ordered orange tuxedos for all of the groomsmen based on the sizes of the black tuxedos that they would all wear when they were at the church. Charley's powder blue, of course, was part of the package.

In order to pull this big surprise off, they kept the secret between themselves and Stacy's sister Jenny. On the big day, November 29, 2008, everyone looked extremely proper in their freshly pressed black tuxedos for the traditional and beautiful church ceremony. They took scenic pictures both in La Jolla and in San Diego.

Then the wedding party rejoined the group at the hotel for the cocktail party. It was then that each member of the wedding party snuck away to assemble for their entrance before dinner. The men received orange tuxedos and the women orange boas. Charley changed into his powder blue. The bandleader made the announce-ment for their grand entrance, and they all proceeded slowly into the ballroom to some very surprised and shocked guests. They made quite an entrance with a wedding party of fifteen all dressed in orange and Charley in his powder-blue tuxedo and top hat. The entire room went wild! There was laughter, and cameras started flashing. The bandleader finally had to tell the guests to sit down and eat. This prank set the tone for a wild and fun wedding reception.

Stacy and Charley danced all night. Their first dance was to Jack Johnson's "Better Together," a very romantic song. With the party now in full swing, the Chicken Dance was also mandatory because Stacy grew up with it at family weddings. "Super Charger" was played too because the happy couple are both big Charger fans. By this time, two of the nieces were on stage with tambourines, and people were singing along with the band. It was an incredibly memorable evening that lasted into the early hours of the morning.

Almost two years after their wedding date, Stacy and Charley welcomed Claire JoAnn to the family. Her slightly late arrival was perfect timing because Charley was not away touring. Their second daughter, Katelyn, was born at the end of July 2013. Stacy opted to have an induced delivery a week early to make sure that Charley would not miss the birth or cut it too close. He was just in from Canada, and that would allow him one full week off before he would play in the PGA Championship. It is a little bit tricky timing babies with the golfing season.

Claire received her first set of plastic golf clubs when she was three from the Easter Bunny. When Charley took her to the course with her first set of kid clubs, she liked to play, but driving the golf cart and visiting the woman who sells snacks on the course was more fun. When Katelyn was little, she liked putting the ball into the hole. The girls traveled with Stacy and Charley and watched their father and other friends' dads on TV. Being so young, it was hard for them to watch more than a couple of holes in a tournament. They both had a lot of energy and short attention spans.

The Masters Tournament in April 2015 was the first time Claire (age five) and Katelyn (almost three) put on the traditional coveralls and did the kids' round of golf. They loved it. Claire also enjoyed the daycare at the Masters because she could wear flip-flops and got to do pretty much anything she wanted. (The tour daycare requires closed-toe shoes.) She even told Stacy that she wanted to move to Georgia and go to school there because of all the freedom and attention.

As Stacy tells it, when you are married to a professional golfer, it's easy to lose your identity. At first, she started out as Charley's girlfriend, then became Charley's wife, and finally the mother of Charley's kids. Once Stacy heard through the grapevine that one of the volunteers in transportation had bragged, "I know the Hoffmans. I drove Claire Hoffman." Claire was two-and-a-half years old at the time, and Stacy had definitely been in the car. The volunteer remembered that Claire sang and talked a lot. All he remembered about Stacy was that she was "Mrs. Hoffman."

Stacy says, "I am just a normal girl who fell in love with a guy who golfs, and now we make the road our home for most of the year. As cheesy as this sounds, your home is where your family is." She always tried to make things special for any holidays that came up. "I love holidays!" she says. "For Valentine's or St. Patrick's Day, I picked up paper plates and napkins and brought special treats to the daycare. We made Valentine's Day cards. We did things as if we were at home." It was also important to be around other families with kids around the same age and similar interests. Stacy got to know a lot of the players and their families, which helped with being on the road so frequently.

Another big help was the caddie and his wife, who pulled a trailer to most of the tournaments, filled with bins for families so that they could transport toys or other large items. Claire always had her own special step stool so that she could wash her hands or brush her teeth at the sink. Katelyn had a little chair so she could eat in the room.

Stacy and Charley were strict about no electronics at the dinner table. Instead they brought stickers, coloring books, and other things to entertain the children while dining out. Sometimes they ran into friends with kids who had an iPad at the table. Claire would try to buddy up, saying, "What are you watching?" That was the exception.

Most often, they used the time as family talk time.

When Claire was young, she managed to close the door to the adjoining hotel room, and it locked. That was a scary moment. Fortunately, the hotel manager sent someone up quickly to open the door. For the girls, sleeping in portable cribs and playing in a closet was normal. Even at home, Claire would say, "I'm going to put my baby doll to bed" and then walk right over to the closet. Family time has always been precious to Stacy and Charley, so they did their best to maximize their time together and make life on the road fun.

Charley always said that his job was easier when they were on the road. Stacy had to deal with entertaining little children in hotel rooms. It was challenging if the kids were sick or when the nap times altered due to time changes. Trying to console little ones late at night or early in the morning could be difficult, especially if Charley had an early tee time. Stacy found that she gave in to the kids a little more than she ordinarily would have. But she was amazed when she discovered that Claire developed early on the skill of getting to the bathroom when she needed to in the middle of the night, especially because each hotel room is different. The girls did an amazing job with all of the traveling.

Charley also became an expert packer. With two car seats, a stroller, and golf clubs as part of the essential equipment, packing in one suitcase became paramount—you never knew how big the courtesy car would be. When the caddie trailer items arrived, they could make the hotel room their home.

Both Stacy and Charley were raised to believe family is so important. Once the girls were in school, they tried to travel together as often as possible. Stacy has always appreciated how hard Charley works at his profession, and she reminds him to this day that he gets to do what he loves practically every day. She tells Charley, "As long as you are doing what you love and can pay our bills, then I'm all for it!" He still loves to play.

Stacy never did learn to play golf—it's Charley's profession, and she would not be able to compete. If she had played before they met, things might have been different, but that was not the case. Instead, the two spend their "couple" time together going to concerts, baseball games, and other sporting events. Going to the beach, camping, snow skiing, and anything water-related are fun, too.

The first time Stacy played in the PGA Tour Wives Classic prior to the Waste Management Phoenix Open was in 2015. She didn't even take lessons. "We never even practiced!" she says with a laugh. "We just showed up, and it was a lot more fun than we both imagined." How did she learn to even hold a club? "I just sort of did it. I have watched golf for so long, I just knew. Sometimes I made contact with the ball and other times I did not." Charley was her caddie, and they laughed a lot that day.

Stacy is Charley's biggest supporter, no matter how he is playing. She tells him, "I love you no matter what." Golf is his career, but unfortunately, it is a very public job. The players are very competitive, so there are both good days and bad days at work. Each player wants to win, and that makes them strive to be amazingly good at what they do. Charley for the most part leaves the golf on the golf course, and Stacy's job as Charley's partner is to be as supportive as she can be. Stacy knows she cannot control what happens on the course. She wants him to do well because he works so hard, and winning makes him happy. Their two daughters also keep Charley grounded and always make him smile.

When they celebrate a win, it can be doing something simple. In November 2014, Charley won the OHL Classic at Mayakoba in Mexico. The entire family and his caddie, Brett Waldman, went to a little taco restaurant. Stacy enjoys seeing Charley so elated when he wins and knows it opens up so many opportunities for him to play with the best of the best. One honor that comes every other year is the Presidents Cup, which is a series of men's golf matches between a US team and an international team representing the rest of the world minus Europe. Europe competes with the United States in the Ryder Cup. The possibility of being on the Presidents Cup Team became a reality for Charley in 2017, and with that accolade came a big celebration.

Stacy does not like to wear her badge identifying her as a player's wife. It not only draws too much attention, but she may get asked technical golf-related questions, and she might not know the answer. She and Charley keep the golf separate from their relationship. Sometimes, of course, people do not realize who they are standing next to. She has overheard some comments, especially when Charley's hair was longer. They would say things like, "He must be a hippie, or a surfer," or "He must smoke a lot of weed!" Stacy ignores these comments and assumes they do not know any better. One male fan in Houston, who had long blond hair and was dressed up like Charley, had asked to take a picture with him.

Stacy says, "Because of what the players do on TV, people talk about them. They are really just normal people who are really good at something." Also, because so many people play the sport, they think they are experts. She often hears comments like, "I can't believe he did that." In baseball, football, and basketball, the fans are in the stands. The players typically do not hear all the chatter and comments. That is not the case with golf.

Stacy never realized how good Charley and the other pro golfers were as players because she did not play the game. After attending a pro-am tournament at Pebble Beach, she was enlightened as a ball from an amateur flew into her direction while she was standing on the cart path. Occasionally, a pro will hit poorly, maybe one or two bad shots. When amateurs are playing, those odds increase significantly, and you must watch the ball constantly.

Once Stacy started traveling full time with Charley, she became involved with the PGA Tour Wives Association, serving first as media chair and then as vice president of communications on the board of directors. This was a perfect fit because of her experience with national and local media. She felt it was important to change the image of the tour wives and let the public know that they do not just go shopping, have spa treatments, and stay in extravagant hotels. The Tour Wives Association's goal was simple: show how tour wives give back to the communities that they call home each week. Since that time, their goals have expanded with an even broader reach.

Over the past five to seven years, the PGA tour wives have opted to do more hands-on projects. In the past, they would tour hospitals and do photo ops. Now they make more of a difference with projects that directly help children and do other works of charity. One of the programs they help support is Blessings in a Backpack. Many children receive meals during the school week by federal government programs, but on the weekends, they have little or nothing to eat. This program fills that void to give them the necessary nutrition on the weekends.

Stacy and Charley realized how fortunate they both were to grow up with loving and supportive families. They wanted to help children locally in their hometown of San Diego and their adopted hometown of Las Vegas. To accomplish their goal in 2009, they started the Charley Hoffman Foundation. Their mission is to help raise awareness and funds for organizations that provide a positive environment for children to better their future through education, sports, and health.

One of the charities that the foundation supports is Pro Kids in San Diego. Stacy likes the fact that golf is the incentive for the children. After school, the kids go to the community center to do their homework and some community service to earn points. The children can use the points to purchase golf equipment and make tee times on the par-3 course. The game of golf helps build character and teaches values and life skills.

Another favorite charity in Las Vegas is Goodie Two Shoes, which provides disadvantaged children and children in crisis with new shoes and socks. Stacy said that it is so sad to see kids walking around with shoes taped together or an extra pair of socks on in order to make the shoes stay on their feet. It is wonderful to see the joy in child's eyes and the smile on their face when they walk away wearing shoes they chose that fit properly.

Over the past eleven years, Charley, Stacy and their board members (consisting of family and friends) will continue their mission with the maxim, "Think local first." As Claire and Katelyn grow up, both Stacy and Charley will continue to nurture and guide them with the same family values that they were raised with and encourage their involvement in the foundation. Normal people who choose to do extraordinary things truly can make a difference in the lives of others.

10 Male Bonding

At least once a year, Steve goes on a golf trip with his buddies. Sometimes it is with fraternity brothers, and other times it is with other club members.

In our thirty-six years of marriage, Steve and I have found that a little time apart can be healthy. When he goes with the guys, I get to hang out with my girlfriends, and he gets to play a ridiculous amount of golf. Our team shops till we drop, and his team golfs themselves into oblivion—usually thirty-six holes or more per day. If I played golf that much, I would probably have to be buried on the ninth hole of the second round in a sand trap. Good thing I love the beach! Steve and the boys, on the other hand, have a wonderful time betting, playing golf, and drinking—not necessarily in that order.

Steve typically calls me every evening to share that day's events. Sometimes I get the play-by-play; other times he tells me that he has paid for his golf trip because he had a fabulous round and won the pot of money. I'm happy for him, but I know that victory is fleeting.

Golf expenses can really add up. There is the green fee, which is pretty high on the courses he plays. Then there is the cart fee. Then there is the caddie tip, which can get even higher for a walking caddie depending upon their skill level. By the end of the golf round after lunch and liquid refreshment, a golfer could have spent quite a bundle depending on how badly he played and how much he had to drown his sorrows, not to mention after all of that having to pay up his wagers. Older golfers who are retired do not typically bet big. I am thankful for those guys. I don't want to lose the house over a golf game.

Remember the deal when I first married Steve? I would get to spend the amount he spent on golf at some fancy spa. Well, that time has passed. We would be in the poor house if I did.

When the golf trip with the guys is over, my husband comes home tired and usually doesn't want to play golf for at least a day or two, if you can believe it. He shares a few stories, but I'm sure some unforgettable things have happened that I don't hear about, involving swear words and flowing alcohol. That's okay. I don't need to know everything.

It was raining hard on one of his adventures to Myrtle Beach, South Carolina, but that minor inconvenience didn't stop these guys. Steve's friend Jimmy was playing with a set of archaic clubs, and the grips were very slick—a dangerous combination with the rain. When Jimmy launched his back swing to tee off on a par-3 hole, the club flew out of his hands—and right into the adjacent, alligator-infested pond.

Most would declare that a loss, but not Jimmy. Those clubs had been with him a long time. So, he was off to the rescue! He quickly undressed down to his tighty-whities right there on the course and requested that the other guys go on gator watch. He waded in. The pond was murky. After several attempts, he sadly had to leave his club in the deep. His white underwear was now black, so he left that behind as well. (Wonder if anyone ever found it?) Jimmy finished that round mud-covered and commando.

Another thing that I heard (and not from my husband) was that some men bring along a ridiculous amount of hair products and supplies. The men sometimes share hotel rooms and thus have one bathroom. This can be a challenge for women, depending on their beauty routine, but I never thought men would have the same problem. I was told that sometimes the bathroom counters are so covered with all sorts of products and gadgets that there's no room left for the roommate's stuff. Not only do hair products take up counter space, but their owners also spend hours in the bathroom doing who knows what. I guess this is something usually only wives know.

This male-bonding ritual is important, as it gives me a good opportunity to do the same with my girlfriends. We often plan these events to coincide with one another. The only thing we can't do is schedule them at the same location. Not enough bedrooms! That's too much chaos, even for Steve.

Most of the time, the guy golf trips take them out of town. However one time, Steve invited the boys to stay at our newly remodeled condo in Florida. I was heading back to Chicago to host a baby shower for my daughter, so the timing at least was perfect. I didn't want to be there to cook and clean for the frat boys, if you know what I mean. I had visited Steve's fraternity house when he attended a college reunion, and my feet actually stuck to the floor. Need I say more? But then I thought about how much damage could be done to our place in three days and two nights.

The only things that were not man-guest-friendly were the white comforters on each bed. They were all dry-clean only, and they wrinkle easily. I realized this after a bad experience with only two relatively well-behaved guests. I had to have the comforter in the one room dry-cleaned twice to get a stain out. And most men don't think twice about setting a dirty suitcase on the bed or lounging on the bed with sweaty golf clothes on.

The easiest thing to do in this case was remove the comforters completely and store them in my closet. Since I didn't want to appear to be a neat freak, I told Steve to blame the fussy bedding on the decorator (even though I had picked out the bedding.)

I asked Steve if he would try to hang out in the man cave, which is the lanai—the enclosed, screened-in balcony with glass hurricane-proof sliders. Most of the things out there are washable and have stain protectors in the fabric, so I don't worry if a little Jack Daniels or beer is spilled. However, if the glass doors are left open, rain could come pouring in or the neighbors could get an earful of their wild golf stories and card-playing antics. While I was gone, my best friend who lives down the street texted to let me know that she didn't see any furniture thrown off the sixth-floor balcony. How reassuring!

The frat boys left, and once I got back, I didn't detect a thing out of place or surreptitiously repaired. Steve even had all the towels and bedding washed and remade for future guests. What a great guy! Or a smart husband—destroying the evidence.

These same guys get together annually. In early 2019, one of them purchased a home at the private golf community of Belfair Country, in South Carolina, where that year's PGA Professional Championship was held. This location was a perfect opportunity to have someone else host the group. It would also help Steve out because it's a nice midpoint for his drive from Florida to our other home in Portsmouth, New Hampshire, with our SUV. South

Carolina would give him a place to stay and a break in the long three-day trip.

The guys were very accommodating and worked around Steve's meticulous plan of driving. He never likes to go through the busier traffic areas like Atlanta, New York, or Washington, DC, during the week. Instead, he tries to work those areas on the weekends. Steve also coordinates a stop in Washington to see our daughter Emily, son-in-law Ben, and twins Luke and Olivia.

Everything was going according to plan, except that the fully-packed and freshly-washed car wouldn't start the day before Steve was planning on leaving. The short version is the car was towed, parts were ordered, more things broke, the entire engine needed to be replaced, and needless to say, no male bonding took place. As for me, I was anxiously awaiting his arrival in New Hampshire for nineteen days. It was way past the ten-day rule.

Steve cheered himself up with the realization that he was going to see these same guys in September at a different golf outing in Myrtle Beach, South Carolina—or so he thought. Toward the end of August 2019, Category 5 Hurricane Dorian ruined his second chance. With a statewide mandatory evacuation in place and flights being cancelled, Mother Nature was clearly winning this golf round.

But sometimes it works out great. The best male-bonding trip ever was when Steve and his buddies headed to "the land where golf was born." Remember that fiftieth birthday gift that had to be put off due to my surgery? It only took seven more years for Steve to get there, but the trip was well worth the wait.

In 2014, Steve and no fewer than sixteen of his golf buddies from Crystal Tree Country Club were primed and eager for their trek across the ocean to Scotland. The head pro, Gabe, and club member

Mike planned the eight-day trip a year in advance, as tee times on these historical courses are booked solid. Most of the courses have a handicap limit—needless to say, I didn't qualify. I was truly okay with this, as this trip would be a major testosterone festival.

It would be nonstop golf for seven days, with endless golf talk and, you guessed it, drinking to fuel the conversation. Scotch is popular; however, most of the boys prefer the pints. If Steve isn't indulging in a Jack and Coke, he'll have a local brewski with the boys. Local pubs are not the place for a martini or a glass of wine.

Most of the boys chose to arrive in Scotland the day before round one of golf, so they found their own transportation to the hotel and to the local pub. Steve, on the other hand, tried to sleep his way to Scotland. He arrived in the morning a little red eyed but beyond anxious to hit the links. Lucky for him, his clubs made the same flight and were unscathed. However, his bag incurred some damage with a bent leg on the stand, which broke off in Steve's hands as he tried to straighten it. (His caddie would later deal with that problem by laying his bag down.) Steve sent me a short email to let me know he had arrived at the airport in Glasgow safely, but I could sense the adrenaline pumping and the anticipation of this long-overdue trip.

A shuttle for twenty was waiting for him; everyone else was already there. It was a big bus for one guy, with a potty included. Steve was soon en route to Turnberry, a tiny village on the Ayrshire coast. The bus wound around the countryside along a ninety-minute journey, with only one stop to pick up the rest of the men at the hotel. The golfers were brimming with excitement, having just polished off a substantial breakfast of eggs, cold cuts, sausages, bacon, assorted pastries, and lots of caffeine. They were glad to see Steve and the big bus.

The men, their luggage, and their ever-important clubs were loaded quickly onto the bus, and off they sped to the first scheduled course. Turnberry Golf Resort is located on the Firth of Clyde in Ayrshire, Southwest Scotland. There are three courses, two eighteen holes and one nine. The men were set to play both the Ailsa and the Kintyre Courses. The Ailsa Course has holes with special names. The third hole is appropriately named Blaw Wearie (Out of Breath)—it's 496 yards of struggle. Number 10 is Dinna Fouter (Don't Mess About), something you shouldn't do in golf anyway. Number 14 is Risk-An-Hope (Risk and Hope). Should you take a risk and hit it, then quickly kneel down and pray for the ball to land safely. The 559-yard seventeenth hole is suitably named Lang Whang (Long Whack). It certainly is!

It was a good day of golf, but Steve was a little fuzzy with the jet lag settling in. Because of the early tee times, bedtime for the boys was relatively early. They played golf games and set up teams like they do in the Ryder Cup. They also did little side bets in their designated foursomes to help fuel their competitive spirits. Steve later assured me that most of the betting evens out, and it's rare for anyone to win big.

The weather was actually quite nice for that time of year in Scotland. It was forty-five to fifty-five degrees Fahrenheit—still cold but without the high winds and rain. Steve was actually pleased that when they played the Old Course at St. Andrews toward the end of the trip, they finally got to experience the blustery, rainy, cold weather known to be typical for Scotland. He wanted to show off the high-tech all-weather gear he'd packed and prove he was as prepared to keep himself warm and dry as any local.

The Hell Bunker on #14 is a place you don't want to visit on the Old Course. It took professional golfer Jack Nicklaus four shots to get out of this living hell sandpit in the British Open in 1995. I'm pleased to say my husband steered clear of this iconic spot. It is fun though to look at pictures of men dangling from their feet held by other players, trying to hit their ball out. The good caddies will recommend hitting backward to get out instead of trying to advance the ball forward. Those stubborn Americans do not usually listen to this sage advice.

One of the most special things about the Old Course at St. Andrews is that it is public. You can actually get a tee time if your handicap is low enough, twenty-four for men and thirty-six for women. I will not be playing anytime soon! Instead, I intend to show up on a Sunday, when the course takes a well-needed rest and is open solely as a public park. You can do most anything that day, with the exception of hitting a golf ball.

Steve remembers many things from that memorable day at St. Andrews. He had a great drive on hole #1—the perfect fairway shot—and then his second shot went right into a pond. He said, "When you play the course for the first time in your life, you have to concentrate on playing the game. It's hard not to think about all of the famous iconic spots that you have viewed countless times on your television and then be in awe of them when you actually see them in person."

Playing the Old Course, considered "the home of golf," was a dream turned into a reality for all of these men. It is considered to be the oldest (six hundred years) and most iconic course in the world with its many recognizable features. Steve has a framed picture of himself and three of his golf buddies standing on the world-renowned Swilcan Bridge that is on hole #18. This bridge was built over seven hundred years ago for the sole purpose of moving flocks of sheep across the Swilcan Burn. Now flocks of golfers move across it for the perfect photo opportunity. Steve said, "As I stood on that famous bridge recalling many of the professional golfers who walked across it, oddly, the thought, 'Why did I hit the ball in the water on hole #1?' popped into my head!"

Carnoustie Golf Links was their final stomping grounds. They played the Championship Course, where numerous professional tournaments have taken place because of its level of difficulty. This course did prove a challenge for the men and Steve too, since it's extremely long. Steve said, "It's ridiculously hard—the combination of lots of steep bunkers and the wind makes every shot demanding. At Olde Florida, if I miss a shot, I have a chance to recover. Definitely not here. There is no forgiveness!" The total yardage for the eighteen-hole course is 6,589 yards for men and 6,136 for the women's tees. The average hole is 366 yards long, with the longest being hole #6, a par 5, at 500 yards with a split fairway. It is safer to go the right fairway because it is wider, but the better line to the pin is on the dangerous, narrow left side (between fairway bunkers and the out-of-bounds fence). It's appropriately named Hogan's Alley because the famous golfer, Ben Hogan, hit his ball in 1953 at the British Open up the risky left side. In all four rounds, he hit his target and won the tournament. For fifty years, the hole was nicknamed Hogan's Alley, but during a ceremony in 2003, that name became official.

The Championship Course clearly provides a golfer with a mental challenge, but a physical one as well. To top it off, there are no carts at Carnoustie—you're walking the entire course! On the eighteenth hole, the Barry Burn (a winding creek) is just waiting to consume your ball, and there is no prayer to hit it out. This one poses an immense obstacle for the second shot as it crosses directly in front of the green. The caddie tip says, "If you better a seven—reward yourself with a drink!"

After that round, the fatigued golfers met at the nineteenth hole (aka the bar) to settle up on bets and compare horror stories or victory shots. Their private bus waited to cart them back to the hotel in St. Andrews for a quick shower and one last dinner out. The boys were tired and ready to head home to their wives and families. With their overstuffed suitcases already filled with stinky golf apparel, it was a challenge for some to find room for all of the souvenirs that they had purchased. Steve bought a few items; among them was for me a handmade sweater ("jumper" in Scottish parlance), two St. Andrews shirts for the grandsons, and a couple of shirts for himself from the famous courses he played.

It was a long flight home. Steve managed a few winks between the food service. As he finally stepped off the plane at Chicago's O'Hare, he said he was thankful there wasn't another damn bunker to get out of!

11 The Caddies

When a caddie gets involved in your game, that is the ultimate. They become an indispensable copilot to navigate the course and your cheerleader, when you need one.

This was the case for me in one of my nine-hole-league championships. Championships are always intense. I want to do well — just like my husband. I usually don't have a competitive bone in my body, but for championships it's the whole skeleton.

Most country clubs have a ranking system for caddies. At Crystal Tree, a rookie caddie is just learning. They have had some training by the club and might not even know how to play golf. Once they know more, the caddie advances up the ranks to a B, then an A, and finally they become an honor caddie.

An honor caddie usually plays golf well. They will read your putts, rarely lose any balls, and know all the hand signals, golf etiquette, and most of the rules. Sometimes honor caddies can even assess your swing and choose a club for you. These are the unsung heroes in my book on the golf course because they are as important as having a decent set of clubs.

If a caddie is not needed to carry a player's golf bag, a caddie known as a "forecaddie" can still be used. The forecaddie travels ahead of the golfers to see where the balls fall. The clubs are then riding with the players in a golf cart. After locating the balls, the forecaddie signals to the players the current status of each shot. Forecaddies are worth every penny of the extra cost, with the total being split between all the players using them. Good ones help speed up the playtime, too. I dread the sideways arm-paddling signal—this means that my ball is in the water. I like to swim, but not for a wayward golf ball.

On championship day in 2002, I needed someone who would settle my nerves and do some coaching. I really didn't want a rookie. I lucked out and was assigned Larry, a young man who came from a golf family and was himself a very good golfer. His two sisters even caddied as well. Larry had caddied for me one other time, when I was playing in a couple's golf event. He was good that day, and I was more relaxed and having fun, so I didn't need the pep talks and the coaching. I had my husband for that.

On the first hole with water, I miraculously hit over the water and made a bogey. Hole #2 didn't go as well, and unfortunately my game continued in that direction. With each poor golf swing, I got more anxious.

One of the rules on championship day is every stroke must be counted. You can't pick up the ball after ten or eleven strokes like they allow on normal league days. When you have to hit over the water and your ball goes for a swim, you must keep trying to get one over. This could mean several lost balls and an extremely high score on a hole.

After screwing up so badly on a hole, how do you recover without your psychiatrist there to calm you down? That is when you rely on your caddie, if you happen to get one with a good personality. Larry was just the man for the job.

The next few holes weren't pretty either. I said to Larry, "Do you want to hit the next shot for me?" This made him smile. I asked him to choose a weapon for me. He handed me a 7 iron and said, "Go for it!"

With his encouragement, I took a swing. The ball landed on the green! I now knew I had a guardian angel with me. The round finally ended. My score was terrible, but at least the round ended on a positive note with a few good holes at the end.

I personally have had some phenomenal caddies and some others that clearly have no interest in the sport and are looking for some easy cash without the work. Sometimes these rookies can be a challenge when they are sightseeing or messing with their cell phones. If a forecaddie is not paying attention to where a ball lands, it could take forever to find. Worse, they could get struck by a ball because they are standing where the ball is going.

One morning, I was playing with my friends Nancy, Mary, and Noreen, with Joe as our assigned forecaddie. Joe seemed eager enough and raced to his position on the first tee, which was on the cart path almost even with the dreaded creek. Miraculously (mostly for me), we all hit our balls just in front of the creek and successfully avoided the dense woods on the right side. We all then had easy pitch shots to the green. A pitch shot is when your ball spends more time in the air than it does on the ground—necessary for this hole, unless we wanted our balls to take a swim.

Two of the balls sailed over gracefully, and two decided to take a swim in the creek. (I am not going to incriminate anyone, including myself!) Those in the water received a one-stroke penalty and could do a ball drop on the other side of the creek. I took a seven on a par 4, not a great start (and yes, I had to take that penalty stroke!).

Joe, we discovered, while doing some basics for us like ball cleaning, had his head elsewhere. Was he thinking about the party he was at the night before? His eyes looked a little bloodshot. After a few holes, the ladies and I decided that Joe was terrible. He couldn't find a ball if you placed it in front of him. But we didn't want to be rude to him as he was only a rookie. A few gentle suggestions were made: When someone is teeing off, pay attention to the flight line in order to find the ball. Don't stand so close to a person putting to create a shadow. Finally, always repair ball marks on the putting green, and fill in any divots on the course. That sounds simple enough, but no, not to Joe. He was there for easy money and didn't want to earn it. The final nail in his coffin was when we all saw him texting on his cell phone. Unbelievable!

Overall, most caddies who last from season to season at a country club are good, and some clearly stand out as excellent. Steve always knows who to choose for his caddie in a golf tournament or a club championship. He chooses well because most of his events last for three days. You would not want a lousy caddie for that long. As for me, the caddie is typically assigned unless I specify to the head pro before the golf round. Usually I get a good one, or at least if I see they are really trying, I am not disappointed.

A dear friend of ours, Mike, learned the hard way about the one-stroke penalty if your golf ball hits your own golf cart or any property you have on the golf course—including your caddie.

Mike and three of his good buddies decided to have a forecaddie for their round. Mike's son, Tony, was an honor caddie, and he often went out with his dad, so he became the forecaddie that afternoon. The day started out no differently than any other—great weather, good company, and a challenging course. The group finished the front nine, with some decent scores, and picked up some sandwiches at the clubhouse to continue the round. They played hole #10 (par 3), hole #11 (par 5), and then proceeded to hole #12 (par 3).

On this particular hole, there is an intimidating ravine separating the tee beds from the green. Buddy John hit his first shot and sliced it into the woods. Forecaddie Tony was right on the job and raced over to locate the ball. But as Tony drew near to the woods, Mike hit his tee shot—badly. Shouting "Fore!" to his son, Mike could only stand there helpless as Tony turned and the ball hit him directly in the chest.

A panicked dad raced over to his son, lying flat on the angled hill, gasping for air.

"Tony, Tony! Are you all right?" Mike asked.

Tony struggled to catch his breath. "Dad—Dad—" he said, clutching his father's shirt, "I just saved your ball from going into the woods, but you have a one-stroke penalty for hitting me!"

In March 2019, another club championship at Olde Florida took place, and Steve fiercely wanted his old title back—not for big prize money, but for bragging rights (although Steve is not one to boast about his golf skills—he has me for that job). This year wasn't going to be a walk in the park, as competition was stiffer. Golfers these days are staying in good shape, even the older ones, by lifting weights and working on their core muscles. Some even hire trainers to specifically target all of the muscle groups used in playing golf. Steve no longer has a trainer, but he does keep himself in good shape by running, and he is always practicing after most of his rounds.

At Olde Florida Golf Club, the championship round consisted of eight players, and the format was match play. They alternate match play and stroke play every year for this particular tournament. Match play is a way to score in golf where the player with the lowest score on a hole wins one point. If a player won every hole, they would score eighteen. Stroke play is when all of the strokes are counted, and the golfer with the lowest score wins.

That player's score might be seventy-two if they parred every hole, for example. There are advantages and disadvantages of each of these scoring systems depending on how you are playing that day. If you have one bad hole in match play and lose the hole, it only affects you for that hole, and you lose the point. If you scored a fifteen on that disastrous hole in stroke play, you probably just lost the tournament.

For this three-day tournament, Steve asked Chris to be his caddie. Chris has caddied for Steve for all of his tournaments at Olde Florida since 2013, and he has been a caddie there for fifteen years. He knows the course and could practically walk it blindfolded. Steve appreciates Chris's skill of reading a green to assist him in making that crucial putt and knowing the distance the ball will go with each different club, if struck properly. Steve prefers to walk the course for some exercise with Chris carrying his golf bag, like the professional players. Walking often helps a player relax and get into a rhythm of their game.

Steve succeeded in winning his first two matches Friday and Saturday to make it to the final day of play, the club championship round. He was now playing with his friend, Guy. On any given day, either Steve or Guy could win. They are almost equally matched, although when Guy has been training, he can outdrive Steve by fifteen to twenty yards per hole.

Guy's caddie is Jeff, another excellent caddie because of his knowledge and skills. I observed this firsthand when I arrived for the final nine holes of the championship on Sunday. At 10:00 a.m., Steve and Guy were getting ready to make the turn on the back nine.

Guy was up by two holes, which made me nervous. Lucky for me, Bill Fox, an eighty-two-year-old with a kind and gentle soul, offered me a ride in the golf cart. I quickly accepted and jumped in to see the action.

Steve won the next two holes, which made me think I was his lucky charm. The match was tied. For the next few holes, they kept tying, until Steve pulled ahead by one on the fourteenth hole. I thought this was the break he desperately needed.

After watching five holes played, I noticed that Guy's caddie, Jeff, would constantly say to Guy, "Slow down; take your time." He didn't speak it softly either. This began to irritate me, along with the way he was lining up Gary's putts. I thought to myself, *Is Jeff going to dig a trench to the hole so Guy's ball will just roll down the trough?* When Steve lost the next two holes, those two things started getting on my nerves big time. I wanted to shout, "Guy already knows to slow down and take his time!" (After the tournament was over, I found out that Guy gave his caddie those specific instructions, which were followed to a tee.)

The pressure was immense for me as the wife, just sitting in a golf cart observing. There was nothing I could do. Maybe I could throw a golf ball or a club at someone, or perhaps make a loud noise during a back swing? No, that would be rude! And in my heart, I honestly want the best player to win.

I couldn't imagine the intense feelings and nerves that Steve and Guy were experiencing. It was all tied up now at #15. Then on #16, Guy was ahead by one. On #17 it was tense, but they both shot par to tie the hole. Heading into hole #18, the stress was beyond heightened because Steve knew he would have to make a birdie to bring the score back to a tie game. This was Steve's last chance and only hope. If he made it, they would then go into sudden death and replay hole #1.

Hole #18 was 451 yards, a par 4. Steve was sitting pretty and landed close to the pin in two shots. Guy's second shot landed about twenty-five feet away from the pin. It was Guy's turn to putt.

Caddie Jeff surveyed the green by getting down on the ground in the push-up position until finally he had the line. Guy studied it as well and concurred with Jeff. Once again, Jeff said, "Slow down; take your time!" (I was thinking, *Go fast and rush the putt!*)

Guy struck the ball hard, as he would have to from that distance. He knew he had to make it to win, as Steve could easily make his putt and tie him. The pressure was intense not only for Guy, but the rest of the group as well.

The ball had speed, but was it enough to get to the hole? We all watched with anticipation. Slowly, slowly the ball inched forward—and landed in the cup!

My heart sank for Steve, and he was no doubt disappointed as well. He lost by one hole in match play. Even the scores were so close: seventy for Guy and seventy-one for Steve. It was a great match; neither man was willing to cave on any hole. They were both fighting to the end for the title of club champ. You may think the wife who was sick of storing and polishing all of the trophies (okay, I don't polish) didn't want him to take home another silver-plated remembrance, but I truly did.

Some caddies just do the basics: locate balls, clean them, and hand out clubs. The more experienced caddies calculate yardage, read putts, and may even choose a club for the player if they know the player's game well. But caddie Kennedy, a rugged tower of strength and not too many brain cells, if you ask me, takes his job to the next level. When our friend John hit his ball, it shanked to the left and was either in the pond or bordering it. Kennedy soon discovered the ball lying near a four-foot alligator, weighing somewhere in the range of sixty to seventy-five pounds.

Normally, most golfers would say goodbye to their five-dollar ball and move on, but this was tournament play. Relief is allowed, as the rules officials would not want a golfer to be dismembered by a gator. A golfer is allowed to take a drop one club length from the nearest non-danger zone, no closer to the hole.

John knew that if the gator wasn't there, he would have an easy chip shot to the pin. Cussing at the gator and throwing a few scuffed water balls at him didn't help. They tried everything to lure the gator away from the ball, but that gator was content lying on the bank soaking up the sun. It was nap time.

After surveying the situation, there really wasn't an ideal place for relief. Being a full-service caddie, half-crazed Kennedy came to the rescue. He snuck up behind the gator and with lighting speed grabbed him by the tail—only to have the gator turn and snap its jaws just as it was flung into the pond!

Everyone was shocked by Kennedy's stunt. He didn't flinch, as if he had been playing with gators his whole life. In fact, he had been since he was about ten years old.

John didn't make the perfect shot he had envisioned, but it wasn't bad considering he and the other players were still stunned over what they had witnessed. The round was finished, and the news spread quickly not of who won the tournament, but of Kennedy and his gator-wrestling skills. And Kennedy was grinning from ear to ear when John handed him five crisp hundred-dollar bills. Kennedy said, "All in a day's work!"

12 The Key West Adventure

During the second year of Steve's retirement, he and I were spending more than half the year in Florida. It is more relaxing, and I do not miss the snow or the cold weather of the Chicago area. Just thinking about it gives me the chills.

I decided we needed a little mini-vacation that was not a golf destination for a change, so when the opportunity presented itself, I jumped on it. My best friend, Donna, had been dating Chad for several months. He offered to take us all to Key West for a two-day trip on his thirty-two-foot boat. It would take four and a half to five hours by boat. I caught Steve at a weak moment, and he agreed.

We all checked our schedules and picked Tuesday, January 22, to leave. Steve had just finished a golf tournament and was willing to part with his clubs for a few days to make his wife happy. The forecast looked good for boating, so we met at the Naples dock at 8:00 a.m. We purchased a few breakfast sandwiches and several cups of coffee and loaded the boat with the rest of our gear. We even planned to do some snorkeling, so I brought my fins and diving mask along.

It was usually cool in the mornings when boating, so I had worn a light jacket and some Capri jeans. Steve had on a pullover, nylon jacket, and some shorts. Donna and Chad had worn windbreakers and shorts, too. Despite calm weather forecasts, about an hour into the journey gusts of wind began to whip our faces, and the temperature plummeted to sixty degrees. Since the sun was not out, it felt more like fifty. The head seas were five to eight feet. The boat was rocking—and not a gentle lullaby! We were not prepared for this. Donna and I wrapped beach towels around ourselves, and Steve put on his golf rain gear, which proved to be a brilliant decision once the sprays of water were coming onto the deck. Why hadn't I thought of bringing my rain gear?

Sitting in the front of the boat was not an option, unless you wanted to get drenched. I squeezed into the captain bench next to Donna and Chad. Steve sat behind us in a beach chair with his feet wedged against the back of the boat for stability. I think we all thought that it would get calmer, but the rough seas continued. I asked Steve to stop singing the 1960s *Gilligan Island* theme song. I didn't want it to bring us bad karma. You may recall *The Minnow* (a touring boat) set out for a three-hour tour, and then all seven passengers got marooned on a desert island for fifteen years. I wanted a vacation, but not that long!

We were already past the halfway mark, so it didn't make sense to turn around. We persevered through the rough waters. After bouncing around and getting wet, I was excited to see some land on the horizon. Our destination was finally in sight. It took us a while to find our boat slip because there were so many marinas in the area. I was thankful the boat had a "head," the boating term for a bathroom. It was challenging to use because of the rough seas, so I only used it once out of desperation. We docked, and everyone raced for the room of necessity. It felt great to be on land. I was also grateful that Steve did not get seasick.

Key West is very small, and most everyone travels by golf carts. We had a rental delivered to the marina. The challenge was to load it with luggage and still have room for us, but somehow we managed. It was a relief to finally be checked into our hotel room and to change clothing. I quickly realized that I had not packed for cold weather. Our weekend trip ended up being four days, so I would have to rewear some clothes to stay warm and even had to loan out a second pair of jeans to Donna. Lucky for us, Key West was very casual and even a little on the grungy side. Most of our entertainment would take place in the bars. Since everyone there would be fairly intoxicated, making a fashion statement became unimportant.

Irish Kevin's became our favorite after-dinner hangout, starting around eight until midnight. We stayed until one of us cried for sleep, usually me. The entertainment and the atmosphere were great. The bar was packed, but we managed to snag a couple of bar stools with a great view of the stage. It was an ideal location; we never had to wait long for a drink. The blueberry lemonade cocktails went down easy. Steve was drinking his usual Jack and Coke.

This one comedian greeted everyone who walked in the bar the same way. "Hey new people, welcome to Kevin's! Where are you from?" When the response came, "We're from [wherever]," the audience responded, "No shit!" in unison. Jerry had coached us. It did not matter where the new customers were from, the response was always the same. It was funny and unexpected by the new people entering the bar. Everyone was beyond friendly, sharing tables if an extra spot was available. The energy and laughter continued through the night.

Later that first evening, we checked out a specialty dessert place called Better than Sex. They serve unusually decadent desserts and beverages. We ordered a chocolate grilled cheese (Danish brie and dark Belgian chocolate grilled on buttered bread with cinnamon sugar) with a shot of strawberry champagne soup to dip the sandwich in. Amazingly tasty! One of the drinks that we tried was called "Lindsay's Lavender Lipstick." It is a glass of Prosecco spiked with lavender syrup and rimmed in honey—a delicious concoction. We also ordered a "Kinky Key Lime." Steve can never resist Key lime pie in any form because it has always been one of his favorites. This version did not disappoint. The dining room was very romantic, with candle-lit tables amid the décor colors of red and gold. Reservations were a must because there were only fifteen small tables in this restaurant.

I think the bars never close on Key West. In the morning, you will see a few drunks walking the street. As for our group, I think we only lasted till 1:00 a.m. We had planned on leaving the next day, but when Chad checked the Marine Forecast Advisory, the conditions did not look promising. There was a small craft advisory for that day. We voted to stay for one more night and leave early on Thursday morning. Thursday's boating conditions showed a better forecast. I figured we could suffer with another day on Key West. Steve was starting to show symptoms of golf withdrawal, but a few Jack and Cokes later, he forgot about it.

We did a repeat of the day before because there is not much else to do on Key West, and the weather was still too chilly to go snorkeling. I was bummed. Snorkeling around the island is supposed to be fantastic.

Our group was up early Thursday, and we headed to the marina with our luggage piled high on the golf cart. At this point, we were all pretty exhausted and just wanted to get home. We had enough fun on Key West, also known to us as Gilligan's Island. We boated out about five miles, and the conditions were miserable. Once again, Steve started humming that TV show's theme song. We were getting pelted with waves and getting bounced around. The waves were now between six and ten feet—no smooth cruising for us. Captain Chad made the decision to turn our "*Minnow*" around. After a short discussion, we came up with plan B: dock at the marina, rent a car, and drive home. Donna and Chad would return to retrieve the boat when the weather conditions were better.

With more than thirty-nine bridges to cross and one break for lunch, the drive home took us close to eight hours. We found a great little restaurant that served buckets of fun beverages. Poor Steve had to pass; he was the designated driver. Chad and Donna fell sound asleep in the back seat with smiles on their faces. I was trying my best to stay awake, but I would occasionally doze off. The drive seemed endless, as the speed limits in certain areas were only forty mph. Bridge after bridge brought us one step closer to home. Donna and Chad never woke up until we were at their door.

Everyone was thrilled to be home at last, especially Steve, as he was experiencing golf withdrawal. It will be a long time before I'm able to convince him to do another boating adventure, as we did feel somewhat marooned on the island.

Short vacations like this are wonderful, as they provide a necessary break from work, daily living, or, in our case, golf. The new activities energize us as a couple. It's great to experience different adventures: trying unusual foods, exploring a new city, and, my favorite thing, meeting new people. Over the years, many former strangers have become good friends. While Steve might not agree, there is more to life than golf!

THE RULES OF THE ROAD:
SARAH STRANGE

Wacky adventures and unusual experiences are not new to Sarah Strange since she became the golfer's wife—and it all started with her honeymoon. Not many people (besides his own wife) can say they spent their honeymoon with the legendary Arnold Palmer, but Sarah Strange, wife of two-time US Open champion Curtis Strange, is one of them.

Sarah grew up in New Bern, a small town in eastern North Carolina, in the 1960s. Even as a very young person, she always had a heart for using her talents to support worthy causes. When she was only ten years old, Sarah organized the "Pop Poppin Players," pantomiming to the music of *Mary Poppins* for their family and friends to raise money for the American Heart Association. It was so successful and fun that Sarah and her sister put on a circus with their combined friends and donated that money to the AHA as well. (That wouldn't be the last contribution Sarah would make to changing the world.)

When she headed to Salem College in Winston-Salem, North Carolina, in the 1970s, Sarah didn't know that her time there would be short. Curtis Strange was attending nearby Wake Forest University when the two met at a local social event for students. Sarah remembers they had "eyes for each other" and talked most of the night. However, by the end of the evening, he still hadn't asked for her number.

Back at the dorm that night, Sarah's friend asked if she had met anyone, and Sarah responded with an excited, "Yes, I did! I think his name is Curtis." The next day, Curtis talked to the same girl and asked her if she could give him Sarah's number. The attraction had apparently been mutual.

Sarah and Curtis were soon dating exclusively. Although Curtis was on the golf team and played in many events, for the first few months, golf was not part of their conversations. Sarah's brother-in-law, who played golf at North Carolina State University, would ask her, "Are you dating the Curtis who won such-and-such tournament?" She would then ask Curtis, and he would say yes. Her brother-in-law would ask about another tournament and get the same reply. He told her, "Do you realize that you are dating an amazing golfer?" Sarah had no clue of Curtis's skill level.

Sarah and Curtis truly cared about each other even with her unfamiliarity with golf, but as their relationship developed, so did her understanding of the game. She missed seeing him win the NCAA his first year and even the Wake Forest team's win the second year. Unless her parents attended a tournament, she was not permitted. Thankfully, they went to several with her. She explains, "His coach wouldn't allow girlfriends to go." Back then, coaches thought even seeing your girlfriend while playing would distract you from your best performance.

After completing his junior year at Wake Forest, Curtis decided that he was ready to leave school and turn pro that summer. By this time, Sarah had attended Salem College for two years and decided to switch from training as a designer to planning a future with Curtis. They talked about marriage and life on the tour.

On the evening of the US Bicentennial, July 4, 1976, at her family's river house in Vandemere, North Carolina, Sarah and her parents watched televised fireworks from New York. Curtis was in England but called to wish Sarah a happy holiday. He also said to her, "Just go and tell your parents."

He had proposed to her earlier, and she had accepted, but they hadn't yet said anything to their families, hoping they could do it together. He was missing her on his travels, though, and didn't want to wait any longer to get married. Sarah responded, "Oh, okay!" She let her parents know, informally, that night, that they had plans to marry.

When Curtis returned a week later, he and Sarah gathered with her parents for dinner in New Bern. Everyone knew that it was supposed to be the night of the "official" engagement announcement. It was a little quiet at the dinner table. Everyone ate slowly, anxiously waiting to hear the big news. It never occurred. The table was cleared, and the leftovers put away. The four of them adjourned to the living room, where they watched television. Finally, Sarah's mother could not wait any longer. "It's getting late," she said, "so I am going to bed." Sarah's father got up to go with her. Then suddenly Curtis blurted out, "Sarah has something to tell you!" Everyone broke out in laughter.

Their engagement was only from July to September. "He wanted me to go with him to the tour school that fall," says Sarah. He had already turned pro, but he didn't have his card. "He had some tournaments lined up and didn't want to go alone." Sarah laughs about the short engagement now. "My mother was going, 'I don't think we can pull this off!'"

But all the plans fell into place, and they were married Friday, September 24, 1976, at the Christ Episcopal Church in New Bern, with a reception at her family home.

The honeymoon night was in Washington, DC, at the Watergate

Hotel. The very next day, Curtis was scheduled to play in an exhibition with his mentor and friend, the golf champion Arnold Palmer. Curtis had gotten to know Arnold because he went to school on the Buddy Worsham/Arnold Palmer Scholarship when he was at Wake Forest University. Arnold had taken Curtis under his wing; both were with the same management company, and they had become close friends.

So that's how it was that the day after her wedding, Sarah found herself on a private plane piloted by none other than one of the greatest and most charismatic players in golf history. "Literally we got married on a Friday," she says now, "so Curtis could play in an outing on Saturday with Arnold."

The only problem was that Sarah had awakened that Saturday with some aftereffects from celebrating their marriage. Arnold, known back then for his adventuresome piloting skills, enjoyed buzzing golf courses when he flew. Normally everyone found this fun, but this time Curtis had to say, "Mr. Palmer, we had some champagne last night, and Sarah doesn't feel so good." Arnold understood. He moved her up to the front of the plane, where she could enjoy the flight. Sarah and Curtis stayed with Arnold and his wife, Winnie, that night in Latrobe and many times over the years during the Arnold Palmer Bay Hill tournament and the Latrobe Classic—Arnie's Army. Their relationship, with so many fond memories, is truly cherished.

After that trip, she and Curtis left for six weeks and literally flew around the world so that Curtis could start his career. One of the first stops was in Belgium. The plane then had to stop in Russia to refuel on their way to their next destination; Curtis and Sarah were the only two people who did not get off the plane. Sarah was fearful that the Russian security would not allow them to return to the plane—it was the 1970s, the height of the Cold War. They then went on to Indonesia and spent three weeks in Japan and one week in Australia.

Sarah was thrilled to have some other golfers and wives from the states finally join them in Japan. Their own budget was very tight, so the meals typically consisted of McDonald's and Kentucky Fried Chicken. Sarah even did all the laundry in their hotel room and had to hang it everywhere to dry. The following year at that same hotel, there were signs in the rooms saying, "Do not do laundry in the room!" Sarah is certain that she caused them to make the sign.

The last tournament of the six-week tour was in Australia. Curtis played extremely well that week and came in second to Jack Nicklaus. The purse was significant—enough to pay off some loans and help them gain their footing financially. Once home in the US that December in Brownsville, Texas, Curtis tried to get his tour card. He missed it by only one stroke. This was a time as a young couple when they did not know if the sun was going to come up the next day. Neither one of them had finished college, so they were not always sure how they were going to make ends meet.

But even though Sarah was a complete newcomer to golf when she started traveling with Curtis, she dove into the life with all she had. "If I went back and did it now, I would take advantage of the places we were able to go. But," she says with a laugh, "I had just been married only six weeks—I had all my thank-you notes to write!

"That first six years of the tour, until we started our family, it meant so much to me to be able to be there with him as his wife," she says. "At the time, I went strictly wherever he went. I went to the golf course and sat and watched him hit balls. I just was always with him." She had a lot to learn. "I would come back after a tournament and ask him simple questions like, 'Explain to me why you did this,' or 'Why did that player do that?' It was a huge learning curve."

Luck was on their side; the next tour school was at nearby Pine-hurst in North Carolina in June of 1977. This was a course where Curtis had proven his skills and been successful. He won the North South Tournament twice there and loved the place. Curtis played phenomenally and received his tour card in 1977.

After Curtis earned his tour card and started traveling on the circuit, in order to save money, they would share a car from Rent a Wreck with other new golfers, like Phil and Kitty Hancock. Sarah recalled one instance when the husbands were under the hood holding some wires together while she was in the driver's seat with one foot on the gas and the other on the brake. The men would slam the hood down and jump in, while Sarah would quickly slide over. With lots of luck and a few prayers, the car would stay running until they made it to the course.

In Milwaukee at a small motel, the room rates were hourly, but they stayed there for the week. Sarah was sitting on the little patio outside her room in a terry-cloth sun suit relaxing when a maid came up to her and said, "Does your momma know where you are?" Sarah replied in a meek voice, "Yes, I just talked to her a few minutes ago." Then the maid spotted her ring, and Sarah said, "Yes, I'm married." She had not realized what kind of a "motel" it was until after she noticed all the big Cadillacs going in and out of the parking lot.

Jan and Peter Jacobsen also stayed with them at that motel. They cooked together almost every night. Jan had an electric skillet, and Sarah had a Son of Hibachi portable grill and a cooler. Sarah says, "You can only eat so many hotdogs!" The other important thing on the road was to scout out a laundromat. No one wanted a repeat of the laundry fiasco in Japan. It was all very challenging in the beginning, but Sarah and Curtis did what it took to make it work.

Sarah never regretted not having a career of her own once she was married to Curtis, even though she had been going to college. "I was so in love with him. That's just what I was going to do. I didn't know what was in store for me. You're just working along until he starts to play better and sometimes win. Before that, it had been a real leap of faith."

Sarah's faith in Curtis ran deep. "I'm sure my parents were thinking, 'Oh my goodness.' Back then, even though you had your card, you had to get into each tournament. There were a few invitations, but if you didn't get one then you had to qualify on Monday's round. If you did not qualify, you were not in the tournament that week. Once you qualified, you still had to make the cut, which would be on Friday in order to play on the weekend. If you did not make the cut, you did not make any money—you spent money that week. You had to pay your caddie, hotel, travel, expenses, and food. We would try to survive on fifteen dollars a day for food. We did not stay in nice places. You do what you gotta do. In fact, we chose to sell my car to have some money to live on."

The first big tournament that Curtis won was Pensacola in 1979. Sarah's mother and father were there to share their excitement. At last, Sarah and Curtis experienced enough financial relief to begin feeling a sense of security. In 1989 Curtis won his final victory on the pro tour. He had a Hall of Fame career throughout that entire decade.

"It makes you work really hard and be very careful," Sarah says. "You start playing pretty well, and before long we had a condo in Kingsmill, Williamsburg, Virginia. We could get a little more furniture here and a little more furniture there." Curtis toured from that location. "Later on, we were able to buy a little house, and after we were married about six years, we were blessed to be expecting a baby. It was wonderful to have that time frame that was just the two of us when we could truly do what we needed to do—build our relationship and concentrate on that part of his career. We're very fortunate the way things progressed for us."

Sarah has said in the past that the golf life is quite unpredictable. Although it probably goes without saying, the best way to succeed at it is to play well. Playing well means you take home a good paycheck, and you can get stability. "So that's a heck of a lot of pressure on the player," Sarah says. Did they have a plan B if the playing well didn't work out? "No. This was what he wanted to do, and I supported that."

Their two sons were born right at the height of Curtis's career, Thomas in 1982 and David in 1985. Although traveling on the tour with a toddler and a baby presented challenges, Sarah's creativity helped her out. When they went for a trip, she created a "Santa Claus sack" for the baby equipment. She used heavy quilted fabric a car seat, stroller, diapers, and toys, and checked this large item at the airport. (With today's airline luggage standards, no one could ever get away with this.) She did not have a portable crib for David, so she would take out a dresser drawer at the hotel and fashion a makeshift one. She never hired a nanny but occasionally had a babysitter or a niece to help on the road.

Once when they were in Palm Springs for a tournament, they stayed in a condominium. To Sarah, this was like heaven. She had two bedrooms, a kitchen, and—the best part—a washer and dryer. When they arrived, little Thomas had intestinal flu but was showing some improvement, and David appeared fully recovered. That afternoon, Sarah became the next victim to succumb to the nasty flu bug. She was so ill, she could barely move. Curtis walked in the door only to discover his wife lying motionless on the couch. She said, "Please, just take the boys out and get a pizza."

Curtis didn't hesitate to follow the request and headed out the door with two little boys in tow to Pizza Hut. They ordered, and a short time later, a large cheese pizza was set on the table. David took in the smell of the sizzling cheese; he barely had a bite before being overcome with nausea and lost it! With reflexes deeply honed through years of athleticism, Curtis grabbed David and carried him like a football in a race to the bathroom. When Curtis finally returned home, all he could say in an exasperated tone was, "Sarah!" She responded, "Do not talk to me—I am so sick!" They both still laugh about this story.

When the boys started going to school in Williamsburg, Virginia, Sarah would stay home with them, but occasionally they would all go on the road with Curtis. The children would get their school assignments for the two weeks they were traveling in order to keep up, and they always did an extra report on where they went. The teachers were extremely helpful. Sarah would get the boys to knock out the assignments in a couple of hours in the morning. Then in the afternoon, they would check out the museums, zoos, and many other places of interest. Traveling to Australia was a wonderful adventure for the boys, one that they will always remember.

Sarah was fortunate that her parents would come and take care of the boys when there was a major tournament or a few special tournaments that she wanted to attend. It was wonderful that the boys had bonding time with the grandparents, and she and Curtis had some time together. When the boys were in high school, Sarah didn't travel much on weekends, except to the major tournaments. Instead, she attended the boys' games and met their dates, not wanting to miss anything. "You need to be there for your children!" she says. Curtis always tried to maximize his family time by coming home from a tour on a Sunday night and back out on Tuesday afternoon. During this precious time, he did not want to miss any of the boys' sporting events. Thomas and David were thrilled to have their dad home and attend their games. Frequently, Sarah would surprise Curtis with his favorite pot roast dinner that he could smell cooking as he pulled into the driveway.

Golf as a sport was never forced on the boys; in fact, it was played down. Instead, Sarah and Curtis encouraged all sports. The boys played soccer, baseball, basketball, tennis, and lacrosse. They wanted the boys to try them all. Sarah and Curtis had played tennis when they were dating and even played with Sarah's mom and dad. Curtis was a natural athlete—he would make Sarah so mad when she hit the ball to his backhand, because he could just throw the racket into his other hand. Tennis became their family sport, and they played it even when they took a vacation. Water sports became another option that the family all enjoyed. Many hours were spent on the James River either fishing or water skiing. Deep-sea fishing became a family event, as they would all crew and cheer Curtis on to catch the big one. Sarah even took over the helm so that Curtis could reel in an amazing blue marlin. After the quick photo, the marlin was free to go.

Still, sometimes Curtis would take the boys out to the driving range and give them some pointers. And sometimes they would all come home frustrated with each other. Sarah would have to tell them all to go to their rooms and calm down.

Raising boys when Dad was often out of town also had some challenges. One time long before cell phones, high schooler Thomas wanted to go to a concert at Virginia Beach with some of his older friends. He had it all worked out, but Sarah did not want him to go, nor did she want to shoulder the decision alone. She wanted to talk to Curtis in order to present a united front, but Curtis was in a pro-am tournament. Sarah called the course to talk with the tournament official; she thinks it was Jon Brendle. "Jon," she said, "this is Sarah Strange. Do you know what hole Curtis is on?" When Jon responded with yes, she told him her dilemma. He then hung up and hopped in a golf cart to get the message to Curtis. "Sarah wants to know if Thomas is allowed to go to a concert in Virginia Beach," he told him. The answer was a definite no, and everyone there burst out laughing.

The Father/Son Challenge was a big deal. Neither Sarah nor Curtis wanted to expose their sons to the media at an early age, so it was not until the boys' college years that they started playing in this event. When one son was playing with their dad, the other son would caddie for the brother. It was also a highlight to see other sons and daughters who they grew up with play with their fathers. This was always a very special event for the family to enjoy together.

In the forty-four years that she and Curtis have been married, Sarah herself never really took up golf. At one point, Joy, her friend in Morehead, had been after Sarah for some time to play nine holes. Sarah finally relented and, surprisingly, played well—wearing tennis shoes—even though when she pulled out her clubs, they actually had a little bit of mold on them. Before she started their round, Sarah spotted Curtis on the practice range, so she requested a mini lesson. He placed her hands on the driver, and she did not move them until after hitting the ball on the first tee. The round of golf went so well that Joy thought Sarah had been secretly playing without telling her. After the round was over, Sarah found Curtis. She said, "Get in the cart, and listen about my nine holes for a change!" He then treated the girls to a celebration beer.

When Curtis played, he did not have to tell Sarah how he did because she was almost always watching. If she was not at the tournament, she followed on TV and eventually online. By doing this, she could anticipate how the later phone conversation might go. She learned what to ask and most importantly what not to ask. She says now, "You may have to talk about something totally different."

Sarah got more nervous watching Curtis play on television than when she was there in person—she couldn't do much to help him over the airwaves. When she was on the course, Curtis could always walk over and talk to her if he wanted. It turned out that he kept an eye on her, too, as much as she was watching him. He would often amaze her by always knowing where she was and what she was doing, because he would ask her things like, "Who were you talking to on #14?"

One time when she was watching on TV and Curtis was in the lead, Sarah tried to distract herself by chopping vegetables. But the tournament distracted her instead, and she cut her finger so badly that she had to go to the hospital for some stitches. She will even do some ironing when watching on TV but admits Curtis irons better. When he wants it to look "right," he does it himself.

Sarah has never paid attention to golf stats or the ranking of a golfer on the money list. She finds that it is not helpful. She wants Curtis to do well for his own satisfaction and enjoyment of the game. In 1985, Curtis was at the Masters in Augusta. It was an exciting time for the family because David had been born the week before. With a young infant, Sarah couldn't go to Augusta, but Curtis's mother, Sarah's father, and other family members were there. Curtis shot an eighty on the first day, followed by sixty-five and sixty-eight, and with nine holes left to play on Sunday, he had a four-shot lead. It was extremely exciting—until his ball went in the water twice, on holes #13 and #15, during the last round on Sunday.

"Any other time, it would have gone to the green," Sarah says.

"But he was going for it. And there I was with a brand-new baby in my arms just having to watch it on television. I wasn't able to be there for him, and it was a humongous heartbreak. I just couldn't believe it. You can't explain what you feel inside because you know what it means to him and how badly he wanted it."

It was very hard to watch, both in person and on TV. The chance of winning his first Masters Tournament was snatched away in two shots. Sarah remembers Curtis coming home and pulling the car into the garage. She walked over to him as he came into the house and gave him a hug. They both collapsed to the ground and cried in each other's arms.

Sarah is grateful for the support he got from other players. "He had a ton of support from several players of wonderful stature who encouraged him, saying, 'This will either make you or break you.' It gave him great hope and encouragement that people would say things like that to him."

It is still a heartache, but it didn't break the determined Curtis. He went on to win two US Opens back to back, in 1988 and 1989. He was voted Player of the Year in 1985, 1987, and 1988. This special award is given by the Golf Writers Association of America. To qualify, points are given for most money earned in a season and for the top-ten finishes. Then the players vote for the honoree, which makes it so special. Another proud family moment occurred in 2007 when Curtis was inducted into the World Golf Hall of Fame. Sarah couldn't be happier for Curtis with all of these accomplishments.

The US Open wins in 1988 and 1989 bookended another trying time in their lives—Sarah's first bout with breast cancer. She was only thirty-one years old, and the boys were young; her focus was to be there for them and Curtis. It was a frightening time.

Thankfully, the discovery was early and the doctors only had to do a few lumpectomies to achieve clear margins. The recurrence was in June of 2004. She said, "We are done. I am tired of this, and I do not want it back!"

This distressing news came the week of their younger son David's graduation. Sarah and Curtis decided not to say anything to anybody—not right away. Sarah explains, "Our focus was to celebrate with him, then get our arms around it and get a plan set in place. Everybody does it differently, but you have to deal with it yourself. We were just so fortunate at both times that we were able to take care of it early enough." Sarah went for a bilateral mastectomy with immediate reconstruction to help ensure a closure to this chapter in her life. She says, "Now I really want to see my grandchildren grow up!"

Curtis was wonderful and supported her every step of the way. But it impacted him. "After I'd gone through the surgery," Sarah relates, "he just crawled into bed with me. It was me consoling him. The relief I think had come to the forefront for him. I told him, 'It's okay; I'm all right.'" He wanted to be strong until he knew she was fine, and then he fell apart. "The same thing happened at home, when David somehow got a gash across his eyebrow. I was strong and did everything needed—I got him into the hospital with the bleeding. Then the minute Curtis walked into the hospital, I fell apart."

Their connection is genuinely mutual. What they've been through has proven themselves to each other. Gratefully, Sarah continues to be cancer free.

"By the US Open in 1989, we knew that I was going to be okay," she says. "Then, to have Curtis win it again—it was a whole different feeling for both of us to share that. The '88 win felt like a great professional achievement. It was for Father's Day, and he had lost his father at age fourteen. So that win was for his dad. But the next year, we knew it was for us."

That turned out to be the final significant win of Curtis's career. Sarah said, "The press put a lot of pressure on him for a 'three-peat.' It was talked about constantly everywhere we went. But he had won two in a row. Only one other person had done that, Willie Anderson [who won four US Opens, one in 1901, and then three in a row in 1903, 1904, and 1905]. We heard about him all that year." Coming up on the tournament, the press was relentless. "They did the big press conference and everything. It was incredibly pressure-packed. The requests for Curtis's time were constant, and he was trying to balance all of that and the family. It all snowballed. He actually played well and had gotten to a place that he could have possibly been able to pull it off. But it didn't quite happen. We boarded the airplane heading for home. He was exhausted."

The opportunity for Curtis to segue into a television career came along soon after, in the 1990s. He served as a sports commentator for eight years with ABC before he turned fifty. Sarah was glad for him. "It was cool because he would play and then go to the booth, and he really enjoyed that. But I think his golf suffered quite a bit because he wasn't able to give it as much time." In 2001, Curtis had the great honor of being chosen as the Ryder Cup captain for the United States team. However, it was postponed to the following year because of the September 11 terrorist attacks. After the attacks, they were the first team to play outside the United States, and Curtis purposely referred to them as, "The 2001 Team." This was and still is an amazing bonding experience for all of the golfers, wives, and families, since they do so much together in the course of one week. Sarah and Curtis had planned for two years many of the details, from the major details to the minute ones. Choosing the uniforms, meals, and gifts were just a few of the items on the checklist. Sarah said, "As challenging as it was, we tried to foresee everything!" –including having both boys as assistants to the assistants, giving them uniforms and jobs to perform for the 2002 Ryder Cup.

Some great father/son bonding occurred at a couple of British Open tournaments when Tom and David accompanied Curtis to the event. Curtis, the proud father, was in the booth as the course commentator. Sarah was at home watching it all on TV, and knowing all her boys were creating unforgettable memories brought her great joy.

The couple have eased into a life that's gearing up for retirement. "I think in his heart Curtis will say he's still always a golfer, but as time has gone on, he wasn't quite as prepared to turn fifty for the senior tour as he had hoped to be. And now he's sixty-five, and it's okay. He is huge into fishing." In their home in Naples, Florida, Curtis can fish whenever he likes. "He's going fishing this afternoon," Sarah says during an interview. "He can pop out in the boat for a little while. It's a beautiful day, and we just got back in from him doing TV. So, it's a very good time in life. We're very blessed and very fortunate

"We now have four grandchildren and one on the way," Sarah says proudly. "To be able to have time with them and to be part of their lives is just incredible." Both of their sons' families are within a few hours' drive, and they often come to visit at "Camp Strange in North Carolina." "It's so wonderful all summer and fall because here we've got the beach. We've got the water." Sarah loves that each grandchild has their own personality, so she can do different things with each one. They try to have Easter in Florida with everybody each year.

Another aspect of being a golfer's wife that Sarah really cherishes is the friendships they've made over the years. "You know, you go through a period when everybody's raising kids and you might miss seeing each other, but then there comes this time in life that you can reconnect and have all that back. It's just been great. The lifelong relationships that you built are so strong, since they have been through close to the same things you've been through, and everybody is in the various stages of it at various times. It's not only by playing golf, but through Curtis's TV career at ABC, ESPN, and FOX that our friendship circle has expanded even further. We've been so fortunate to have that part of our lives, too."

Sadly, they have also lost some friends as they all have grown older. "We are starting to do some bucket-list things. You think, gosh we need to do some things while we still can."

Sarah in recent years has turned her attention to a cause that is very close to her heart. "My father," Sarah relates, "could have dearly used a hospice house at the very end of his life. At the end, he needed a facility terribly. It wasn't wonderful where we had to take him, and then we had to go chase them down to get the morphine. My sister and I took turns sleeping on the floor and the other staying awake."

In 2003, when Sarah visited a terminally-ill friend, she saw first-hand how a hospice house was beneficial not only to the patient, but to the family as well. When she saw how her friend and his family was helped with an inpatient hospice house, she was impressed. "I had always been involved in the community in some way—for example, doing a golf tournament fundraiser to help the recreation center get the bill paid off for their new building one year and providing free medicine in the clinic for those who couldn't afford it the following two years." Although Sarah didn't know it right away, hospice would be her next challenge.

The need for a hospice house was great in eastern North Carolina; nothing like it existed in a five-county area to help the terminally ill and their families. At that time, Sarah was recovering from her own surgery for breast cancer and had become friends with one of the nurses, Jean Sellers. Jean's entire mission was to get a hospice house in their area. Jean inspired Sarah and encouraged her to form a board to start up a facility.

Sarah agreed to be the chairperson but knew she had a lot to learn. "Through her friendship and helping me after my surgeries, Jean was just the best. We spent a lot of time together. I knew because of her and all that we had shared that I wanted to help do this, too."

When Curtis and three other men started a fishing tournament in 2005 to help raise seed money for the project, things started progressing. The support continued once people started to understand or had experienced a hospice house in other places. "Everywhere we turned, God just provided the right people at the right time. People who at first said no ended up being incredibly wonderful. Mark Twisdale, president of the State Employee Credit Union, laughed and said to me, 'Sarah, you never even heard me tell you no.' I replied, 'No, I honestly didn't. Did you?' He said, 'I guess you're right. I didn't.'"

"It was ten years from the thought of it to opening the doors," Sarah says now. "It started with just me and three others, but the board expanded over time to fifteen members. Each person was a crucial part of the success of the project. Not only did they all give their time and talent, but financially, too." Raising the $5 million needed to complete the facility was their second goal. Their first was to petition the State of North Carolina and jump through many hoops to prove that a facility would be vital to the community. They battled so much negativity; several people said that there would never be a hospice house in Carteret County. However, once the

North Carolina State Credit Union came through with a million dollars, people could see a reality to the vision.

Sarah had never asked for money before, so she had to learn about making presentations. Curtis would sit in the back of the room and give her the signal to stop talking. She would know then that she said enough on that subject. "It was a real turnabout for us as a couple because I'd been there for Curtis whenever he'd had a speaking engagement or a function or this, that, or the other. Now he was doing it for me."

This had become her passion. There were so many stories of families who had the need of this inpatient hospice home. The hospice house allows people to die with dignity and be in a homelike setting, when home is not an option. Many people in the community were willing to help in any way they could. If they could not help financially, they donated their time or their artistic talent; others gave furnishings and many other needed gifts. It was a heartwarming experience and a true labor of love.

The Crystal Coast Hospice House located in Newport, North Carolina, opened its doors in June of 2013. This ten-bed facility is incredible and serves Carteret, Craven, Onslow, Jones, and Pamlico Counties. They have a full staff dedicated to helping the patient go in peace with the love of their family by their side. Sarah says, "You are not treating the illness any longer—you are giving quality to the time left to the patient. It is not only wonderful for the patients, but the family as well. It is truly a homelike environment and a place that offers such dignity, amazing pain management, and love during this very dear and precious time in life." After serving as president for ten full years, Sarah retired at the end of 2013, but her support of this special place, which is dear to her heart, never stopped. In January of 2020, Sarah was excited to return to being on the board, as it was hard for her to stay away. "When you're so invested in it from the early stages, you want to see it to fruition and beyond," Sarah says. "It's very special. People are being blessed."

Sarah's life supporting others and making a difference continues as she enjoys her time with Curtis and her family while promoting the hospice work and pursuing a few items on their bucket list. She signed on early for a life as a golfer's wife, and even with the ups and downs, challenges and triumphs, she wouldn't have it any other way.

13 Like Mother, Like Daughters

Children grow up, and as such, they start to date. When it came time for the dating scene for both of our girls, I teased Steve that he would approve of any guy as long as he played golf. The young man could have a criminal record, be lazy with no ambition, or have a multitude of undesirable characteristics, but as long as he played the game, he would be instantly one of the family! My standards were slightly different, incorporating more of the usual parental sensibilities—Steve only wanted to know the guy's handicap. That's the family joke.

Laura and Emily learned the game of golf when they were ten and nine. We lived down the street from a par-3 course, a driving range, and a "putt putt" miniature golf course. Many family evenings were spent at the putt putt. The girls liked golf enough to try group lessons one summer. I was shocked when Laura came home one day and told me she got a hole in one on their par-3, nine-hole course. However, this achievement was not enough to hold her interest. Golf was too slow for both girls. They preferred tennis. The golf clubs were put in the basement to collect dust.

It wasn't till we joined Crystal Tree Country Club in Orland Park that we signed the girls up for more lessons. They still enjoyed tennis more than golf but were willing to give golf another try. When they both made the high school tennis team, golf lost out again. All their effort went into getting good grades and improving their tennis game. Even golf-obsessed Dad had fun watching them in matches.

Our daughter Laura likes to remind Steve and me that we were blessed with relatively easy teenage girls to raise. They weren't into drinking, smoking, or drugs, nor were they overly boy crazy. Laura did have a boyfriend for a while that Steve called "Spike Boy," because of his hair. His blond spiked hair added at least three inches to his six-foot frame. Thankfully, Laura came to her senses and ended the relationship.

In my discussions with Steve, I told him the best thing would be to remain neutral on our opinions of the boys that the girls brought home—within reason, of course. If you said you didn't like a boy, the girls would hang onto him all the more. By having a neutral opinion or just saying the boyfriend was okay, the girls were able to figure things out on their own. I stand by this parenting tip. As in golf, sometimes you have to try out several clubs before you find the right one to get you to the hole or to the altar. Prayers always help, too! Did anyone ever say this would be easy?

Every once in a while, Laura and Emily would take a break from their friends to appease their parents and play nine holes with us. It could be on a sunny Sunday afternoon or on a vacation. Their favorite thing was to drive the golf cart. On one family trip, Emily swerved just in time to avoid a hedge of bushes. I was in the cart and almost fell out! After that incident, she was known as the "adventuresome driver."

Laura's fate was sealed when she met Brad a few days before Halloween during her junior year at University of Illinois. Laura spotted him from across the street, and one of Brad's fraternity brothers gave him Laura's phone number. Halloween was their first official encounter! He was Maverick from *Top Gun*, and she was a German Beer Girl. The Maverick liked the Beer Girl, and the romance quickly blossomed. When she finally brought him home to meet us, we discovered that he had been playing golf since high school. How did she manage to find a golfer under that Top Gun costume? Steve was happy about that, but we were both thankful that he was also a great guy. Laura even dusted off her old clubs and started playing again. They were married in June 2010. It was good that Steve wasn't retired yet, because if he had been, he would have had to go back to work to pay for the lavish wedding. Three years later their little boy Ian was born. It was very exciting to be first-time grandparents to this adorable baby. Baby brother Jack arrived eighteen months later. Steve and I were hooked. The only thing to do was to relocate to be closer to our precious grandsons.

So, summer of 2017 found us moving from the southwest suburbs of Chicago to Portsmouth, New Hampshire. Suddenly we had to do some repairs to our home in Orland Park for the new buyer, have an estate sale, and decide what could work in our new-to-us, cute-but-tiny home—all of this to close within one month of selling to the first buyer who walked in on day one of the listing. It was an unreal month.

Steve and I barely had the energy to accomplish all this. Countless cups of coffee helped rejuvenate me, but when the clock finally struck midnight, I had to call it quits. Steve's handyman skills saved us some money because he was able to do many of the repairs himself. One afternoon, I walked outside for some fresh air and found him on the roof putting sealant around our chimney cap. We are a team when we have to move heavy furniture, or he shows me his brawny strength by moving it himself. One of our best twenty-dollar investments was some plastic furniture gliders. Those things are amazing with heavy furniture.

I think our new dollhouse residence could be on the HGTV series *Tiny House, Big Living*. I love it because it's easy to clean, it's practically maintenance free, and—the best part—it is only an eight-minute walk to see our two grandsons. Just when I thought life couldn't get any better, Steve and I received the surprising news that Laura was pregnant again. This time she had a little girl, Vivienne Jane.

Of course, Grandpa has taught both boys some basic golf skills. Ian, age eight, and Jack, age six, enjoy soccer more, but both have taken golf lessons through the program First Tee. It's an extra-special time when Grandpa takes them, and the trip to Lago's Ice Cream afterward is an added bonus. Jack will not hit at the range, but he will do some putting. Grandpa Steve totally appreciates their interest in his passion. As for Vivi, three years old, she is still happy being pushed on a swing. Maybe next year.

When Emily's future husband, Ben, asked us for her hand in marriage, he said we could ask him anything. Steve asked what he already knew: "Are you a golfer?" Ben laughed and reaffirmed, "Yes!" Steve responded, "Great! You're in!" We thought he was a perfect match for Emily. They married in June 2013. Steve played with Ben in the father/son tournament in 2014. They took second place and lost by only one stroke.

Like their mother, both girls dusted off their clubs to be with their men and started playing golf again. At least, that is what

Laura did initially when she married Brad. However, since then, with three young children, golf is not in the picture. As for Emily, she gave Ben some private lessons for his birthday and occasionally joins him at the driving range. She doesn't love the game but appreciates the skill needed to play it.

Steve is elated to play golf with his sons-in-law. Over Labor Day weekend 2019, Ben and Emily came for a visit to Portsmouth. Steve booked a tee time for himself and the boys at the Oaks, a public course in New Hampshire, and Steve, Ben, and Brad thoroughly enjoyed their round. Ben played with his new clubs, and Brad hadn't played for a long time, so the father-in-law championed over their youthful age and long drives. There were only a few lost balls, but more were found, and they had a wonderful day of camaraderie. Perhaps in a few years, little Ian will round out this foursome—minus the beer!

Our odds just increased by two for more golfers in the family. Emily and Ben had twins, Luke and Olivia, at the beginning of April 2020. With a full-blown world pandemic taking place, it was definitely a challenging time to have a baby, let alone two. Hospital protocol was in full force, allowing only the mother to see the babies in the neonatal intensive care unit. When they left the hospital without the babies, Emily could only visit once a day for four hours. The anxious father, who had only held each baby once on the day they were born, had to painfully wait at home. It was a glorious day when they finally arrived home and became one big happy family. Potential foursomes, maybe?

When golf is not your source of income and only a hobby, prioritizing what's important in life is a must. Family is a top priority for both Steve and me. We don't want to miss a moment of chaotic fun and laughter with the grandkids and family. Time spent with them brings us endless joy and fulfillment. Neither Steve nor I can imagine our lives any different!

STAY GROUNDED:
KRISTY WEIBRING

"D. A. would always tell me, 'I couldn't do what I do without you,'" says Kristy Weibring, wife of five-time PGA Tour winner D. A. Weibring. "I know he really believes that."

Whether it's your husband or your wife who is well known, Kristy's advice is to be sure to keep them grounded. Remind them that what you have is a gift. She says, "D. A. and I used to say that after something good would happen in his career. When he won the Western Open, as we got out of bed the next morning, I said, 'Okay. Remember our feet are firmly planted on the ground.' I didn't want us to ever be anybody other than who we are."

Her positive presence and unshakable faith—this is what D. A. means when he says he couldn't have achieved what he has without her. "I think we do that for each other," she says. "We are not changing who we are. Just remember, you meet the same people in the same way going up as you do going down, and you better treat everyone with respect and kindness."

Kristy (Jones) Weibring grew up northwest of Chicago, in the town of Palatine, Illinois. She is the second eldest of six children: four girls and two boys. Discipline and love were how her parents raised so many children. Her father did play golf, but she never had any interest in the sport growing up.

"I did not play sports," Kristy says. "When I was in high school, I was in student council as a representative. But when I was younger, I was a cheerleader—for the wrestling team!"

Kristy's relationship with golf started when she met D. A. during their freshman year at Illinois State University. "We really became friends before we started dating," Kristy says now.

D. A. confirms this. "I was attracted to her right away when I first saw her. It's been a great relationship. What I've observed is she's very, very humble. She's very giving and supporting of everybody around her. As time went on when we had children—I mean, she carried the load. I was here; I was there; I was supportive. But she did an amazing job with our kids."

Did Kristy think when she met D. A. that their life together would always revolve around golf? She says, "I didn't go into it thinking, 'Oh gosh, he's going to be playing a tour for forty years,'" she says. "It just evolved."

In 1975, Kristy graduated with a bachelor's degree in elementary education and D. A. with a bachelor's degree in business management. Following college, Kristy taught second grade in the small town of Arcola, Illinois, while D. A. went to Florida to play on the mini tour. He proposed when he came home for Christmas that year. Five months later, over Memorial Day weekend 1976, they were married. Their short honeymoon was a weekend in St. Louis, after which they moved to Detroit, Michigan, where D. A. had a job as an assistant golf pro at Red Run Golf Club in Royal Oak, Michigan, just outside of the city.

Back then, there was a qualifying tour for the PGA every six months. D. A.'s goal was to improve his game and get some financial backing. Kristy went with D. A. to the Brownsville, Texas, tour school

The Golfer's Wife

in December 1976. It was unusually cold and wet that year, and he worked hard to qualify. He was not successful. "It was just one of those awful weather things," Kristy says.

Knowing he was a bit down about not getting his tour card, Kristy suggested that the two of them take a drive across the South. First stop was to see a basketball game in New Orleans, which began to get D. A. out of his funk. Then, in Florida, D. A. participated in a one-day mini tour in January—and he won. That really got him back in the groove. He credits Kristy for knowing just how to get him energized again. "She picked me up after leaving Brownsville. That started the momentum. I needed it at the time," he says. "She is an amazing support to me."

D. A. went on to explain, "That's the role so many wives play behind the scenes. We put on a public face, good and bad, but when we are the most down, we are in front of our wives. Kristy learned the game, and she knew I worked at it hard, but it was her moral support that I couldn't do without."

That victory gave him the confidence to go back to Michigan and continue to improve his game. He told his boss at the club that he felt ready to go to the June PGA school—he didn't want to wait until the following December. The club was very supportive. So, he and Kristy left Detroit to go to the tour school in Pinehurst, North Carolina.

That year, in June 1977, there were over four hundred players vying for twenty-five available tour cards. Back then, to get the privilege of playing on the tour, you had to both get a tour card and then also participate in each of the Monday qualifiers, which had a certain number of spots open to get into the tournament that week. "So, you weren't even automatically in the tournament," Kristy says. "You still had to go through Monday qualifying." Talk about stressful.

But the stars were in alignment for them that year, and D. A. qualified for his first tour card.

In Michigan, D. A. had been working fourteen-hour days. He was at the club from the moment the sun came up until the end of the day. Kristy did a little bit of substitute teaching, but once he got his card, her life and his became about the tour.

Kristy tells it, "We ended up packing up all of our stuff and storing it in Quincy, Illinois," where D. A. was from. "Then literally our home was in our car. Everything that we owned was in the car—our clothes and everything. We drove to all the different tournaments the first two years or so. That's what all the married couples were doing."

In 1978, they bought a house in the Dallas area but still spent a lot of time on the road.

"We picked Dallas," Kristy says, "because D. A. had a first cousin there. He was an only child, too, and they're really close." Plus, of course, Texas is in the South, which meant D. A. could practice almost all year round. Its central location also made traveling—and getting home—that much easier.

They had their first child, Matt, about three and a half years after their wedding, in 1979, but the traveling didn't stop. Kristy says, "Traveling with a baby, formula, and diapers is just what you learn to do."

They built a house in 1981 in time for the 1982 arrival of their second child, Katey, which made traveling even more of a challenge. But believe it or not, the family of four stayed together on the road during the golf season with a customized van, which was like a little traveling house, until it was time for Matt to start school.

Finally, after over eight years of the professional golf circuit living mostly out of their vehicles, D. A. and Kristy settled in Plano, Texas, where they had their third child, Allie, in 1987. Kristy and the kids still traveled with D. A. during the summertime. Summer was their favorite time of year because they could all be together as a family.

D. A. got home as much as he could. "I know that D. A. sacrificed some of what probably could have been an even better career because he wanted to be there for the kids," Kristy says. "He coached all three of our kids in basketball. He always made sure he was there for at least one of the girls' dance competitions in the spring. He flew home one time just to do a father/daughter dance. So, I know he made sacrifices. He is a great dad.

"When our oldest son, Matt, went to kindergarten, I couldn't travel like I used to. I was doing everything at home while D. A. was traveling. We tried really hard for him not to be gone more than two weeks at a time, even if it was him coming in on a Sunday and then going back on Tuesday night. He would just come in and touch base. There were a few times when he would go overseas that he was gone for three weeks, but never more than three weeks. That was just something he didn't do."

Kristy kept the home fires burning. "D. A. always missed being home. He called every night." She laughs when she remembers that the children would always vie for the phone and tell him how much they loved him. They weren't nearly so demonstrative with her! But D. A. would tell her, "Believe me, I wish I was there."

D. A. says, "I would call home almost feeling sorry for myself, in my hotel room. And here she is handling three kids and homework and schedules and all that kind of stuff."

"He would sound so lonesome," Kristy says, "and I was thinking that a hotel room by myself didn't sound too bad!" Kristy adds, "I think that's one thing he doesn't miss. He does not miss the traveling and having to pack up and get all that stuff organized. He enjoys being home. He especially likes when we have all the kids over, and everything is a little bit of a zoo."

D. A. and Kristy's daughters, Katey and Allie, know a lot about the game of golf from watching their dad over the years, but they do not play themselves. Both of the girls decided to dance competitively in high school instead. But they were always super supportive. When Katey was young, she would sit behind the hole when D. A. would practice his putting. He would roll the ball in, and she would roll the ball back to him. One thing Katey would always tell her dad and he would remember when he was playing is, "Concentrate it into the hole, Dad!" That was her line. When daughter Allie was a little girl, she loved to draw. D. A. would call her up before a tournament and ask, "What is my color for today?" Allie would respond, "Hot pink, Dad!" When D. A. would get ready to putt, he would picture Allie drawing a line with her pink magic marker directly into the hole.

The girls left it to their brother, Matt, to be the next golfer in the family. Matt started playing as soon as he could hold those little clubs—there are photos of him swinging away at eighteen months old. Matt also played many other sports growing up: soccer, base-ball, and basketball. D. A. was careful not to push Matt into golf; it had to be Matt's decision. In high school, Matt was an "All-State Basketball Player." He probably could have gone on to play basket-ball in college, but he decided to focus on golf. When Matt went to Georgia Tech, his game continued to improve. In 2002, he turned professional.

D. A. remembers, "Kristy really got nervous watching Matt. That wasn't her husband—that was her son. I would say, 'This will be in-teresting what he chooses to do. He can either do this or he can do that. . .' And she would say, 'That's way too much information for me.'"

"He would want to give me a blow-by-blow!" Kristy says with a laugh. "I said, 'D. A., I have been doing this a lot longer than you have, being a spectator. I can't listen to you telling me everything.'

It makes him feel good because it's his nervous energy. You know, he's nervous, too. And he wants somebody to be able to chitchat to. But I don't want to hear it all. I will honestly say now that D. A. is retired and Matt's not playing anymore, I realize I don't have that constant knot in my stomach. How is this week going to go? What's going to happen this week? You know, that little anxiousness that you have before, when they're going to play, hoping that they're going to have a good week."

Kristy remembers taking Matt as a child to watch D. A. play. When Matt was eight years old, he went with Kristy to watch D. A. in the US Open in Boston. It was Father's Day weekend, and D. A. was not feeling well. He wasn't sure how he would be able to play. But young Matt was there, watching every round. "Here's this little eight-year-old, living and dying with every golf shot," Kristy says. "He would get so excited when D. A. would birdie, and he would be so devastated when D. A. would bogey. He was on an emotional rollercoaster the whole time."

Finally, on the putting green that day, D. A. felt a little tug on his pants. Matt was at his side, with a gift. He said, "Dad, I know you are not feeling very good. Take my St. Christopher medal. This will make you feel better. Keep it in your pocket for good luck!" It was a special father/son moment. D. A. put the medal in his pocket and kept it there through the rest of the tournament, where he not only finished, but also tied for third place.

"Matt felt so bad that Dad didn't win that time," Kristy remembers. "As Matt got older, he got better about it, but when he was really little, it was hard for him to watch. So, D. A. winning in Hartford, Connecticut, is one of my favorite memories." This was the Canon Greater Hartford Open in 1996. Kristy had always wanted Matt to be there for at least one time when D. A. won. That summer, between Matt's sophomore and junior year in high school, he got to be there—and he helped.

He wasn't caddying for D. A., but D. A. often tells the story about how Matt caught up to him in the last round. He said, "Fairways and greens, Dad. Fairways and greens." It was the same advice D. A. would later give to Matt: Take it one shot at a time. Get in the fairway, and then keep it on the green. That day, D. A. took that advice and went on to win the tournament.

Matt has since retired from the tournament circuit and is doing well now in his new career in private equity. "He's made such a great transition," Kristy says. "My husband and I are so thrilled that he's found something that he enjoys doing."

From the outside looking in at these really successful golfing careers, it's easy to think that the person just coasted right through to the top. But Kristy knows that life happens to everybody. Nobody can escape. "Nobody goes through life without stuff happening. You just have to take it as it is."

That Hartford Open win that Matt got to see was also special because it was right after D. A. had returned from a six-week hiatus due to an attack of Bell's palsy, a form of paralysis causing the inability to control facial muscles on the affected side.

"D. A. was going to Florida," Kristy remembers. "I was going to take him to the airport that night, but his ear had been bothering him. I said, 'D. A., don't get on an airplane. Please let's go to a clinic.'" The clinic diagnosed him with walking pneumonia and fluid in his ear, and they recommended that he not fly that night. So, at least he was home when the next phase struck. When he woke up the next morning, his face had fallen.

"It scared the heck out of me at first," Kristy says, "because when I saw him and his face was drooping, of course you think, 'stroke.'

That's what it looks like. For one minute—just a second—I remember thinking, 'Oh my gosh, what if something really serious is wrong?' Then I just shook it off because I didn't want to go there." D. A. had to take that six weeks off to recover, but he bounced back from it well.

Throughout her life with D. A., in the tough times, it has been Kristy's devotion to her Catholic faith that keeps her strong. The family's faith is very important to them. It has especially helped Kristy deal with a spouse who needed to be gone so much and the health challenges their family has faced.

"By the grace of God," she says, "you get through all those ups and downs." When you have that faith, Kristy believes, you don't feel as alone. You feel like you've got a resource you can lean on, even when your partner may not be there.

Not that Kristy tries for an unfair advantage from the Higher Power on the golf course. "I would always pray for D. A. to do well," she says now, "but I wouldn't say, 'Oh Lord, please let him make this putt.' In my mind, I said, 'I know you've got the best plan, and I'm good with that no matter what happens.' It's not always easy to accept it, but somewhere down the road you're going to look back, and you're gonna go, 'Huh. He did have the better plan.'"

Prayer is something Kristy turns to frequently, in the toughest moments. "When something's going on with your kids, to me that's when I pray the hardest," she says. "When something's not right with them, where else do you go with that, but right to using your faith? I probably prayed more about the actual outcome of golf with our son. Your heart hurts more when it's your child. Once he had a wife and then when the kids came along—your heart just twists. It's hard when things don't always go well for your kids. That's when you find your faith."

Kristy's faith helped her with her own anxiety at times, too. "Like I say, I know God has a better plan."

The end of 2009 was another very challenging time. Their youngest daughter, Allie, found out she had Hodgkin's lymphoma, right before her senior year in college. Kristy really had to turn to her faith. "That was something that just stopped you in your tracks. It makes all those little stupid things that you worry about go away." Allie responded well to treatment and has come through it with flying colors. "It's been ten years this year," Kristy says. "And she just had her first little baby. I'm so grateful."

Kristy is philosophical about all that they have faced as a family. "It's through the trials of life—that's how you grow. We've had so many more blessings than bad. I truly feel that way. I feel it in my heart. We have had such a great life."

There have definitely been funny moments, too. On one occasion, Kristy was watching D. A. at the tournament in Hartford 1986 or 1987. He was getting ready to putt using his newfangled 3-Ball Putter, invented by Dave Pelz. It was a special putter designed with three balls attached on the back to give weight and counterbalance to the shot. "It was not pretty," Kristy says, "but it was balanced." Behind her in the spectator crowd, though, she could hear two men talking about the putter. They went on and on about how ridiculous it was and how D. A. was foolish to use it. Kristy fumed as she overheard what they were saying behind her. She finally had enough and turned around—only to see it was Dave Pelz himself! He and his son wanted to see how much they could say before she would come to D. A.'s defense.

That instance makes for a great story, but it's not always fun to hear people talking about your husband on the green. "That's always a hard thing, I think," Kristy says, "for a wife or a family member to hear somebody talking that way. They don't know who you are."

Another time, at a tournament at Westchester Country Club in

New York State, two men were being outspokenly critical as D. A. was teeing off on the first hole on that Friday. He had played well the day before and was hoping to make the cut. These two men right behind Kristy were saying, "Oh yeah, he's not going to do very well," etc. Finally, Kristy turned around. "I was very nice," she says. "In my very sweet voice, I said, 'I really hope not—that's my husband.'" She wanted them to realize there are always people in the crowd who care about the players. "They just felt horrible, I'm sure. But I wanted them to know you've got to be careful what you say. You don't know who's listening." Kristy was especially glad that D. A. went on to eagle that hole.

Another challenge about a job in the public eye is that often you're having to perform right when something in your personal life throws you a curveball.

That's the mental side of the game. It's learning to take it one shot at a time and not to beat yourself up. "I think most athletes would say golf is probably one of the most mental sports," Kristy says. "There's so much in-between time walking. You have all that time to think, 'Oh my gosh, why did I hit it in the bunker?' It's a little game that you have to play with yourself."

A Western Open that Kristy remembers in Chicago was an example of this. D. A.'s father had passed away right about the same time D. A. had begun working with a sports psychologist to learn how to focus, relax, and visualize. It was really helpful to him, and he made no secret about it, even mentioning it in some interviews. But the concepts were still new to him.

"We were only thirty-one when his dad passed away," Kristy says. "We were still pretty young, and it was hard." Initially, D. A. played at the tournament really well. But then a TV announcer walked over and wanted to interview him about the sports psychology. This was enough to put D. A. in defensive mode and to get his mind out of the game. As Kristy puts it, "When you are playing well, you are in a rhythm; you are in a zone. You are in that pocket. Having someone come up and start interviewing him took his brain away." He ended up not playing very well for the last three holes.

"My heart just broke for him," Kristy says. "That's hard to walk out and have to face all those people. He always handled it so well. And the next day, on Sunday, he came back and played really well. I remember afterwards telling him it was one of the proudest moments I had of him because I know that it was so hard to bounce back after that."

D. A. continued his work with sports psychologists, and overall it was very helpful to him. Chuck Hogan in particular had the philosophy, "You get what you think." D. A.'s career is a testament to that.

Kristy herself often found those early years on the tour to be stressful, and she had to develop her own coping mechanisms. Like today, people then involved with professional golf were always talking about the PGA Tour Money List. For the uninitiated, the money list, which is updated and published each week, shows how much a particular golfer has earned from tournaments in the current year. Back in those days, every Monday everyone's earnings for that season were printed in the newspaper for all the world to see. It's like showing the entire world your year-to-date earnings, every week. At the time D. A. was establishing himself as a pro player, rankings on this list determined if players were eligible to play on certain tours or to automatically receive a tour card for the next season. If your ranking changed frequently, it could be very stressful. If you ranked high enough, it meant you automatically qualified for a tour card the following year. If you didn't, well, you wondered if you'd have to start all over again.

"I mean," Kristy says, "that was stress. He had to make X number of dollars in winnings in those first six months to keep his card for the next year. Back then it probably wasn't a lot of money, but to us it was. I think back then it was to try to finish in the top 60, and then you were exempt for the next year." Now it's the top 125.

The thing with being a pro golfer, Kristy says, is, "Every year you start from scratch. Every year! If you had a good year before, it doesn't mean you're going to have a good one next year. I used to think it would be nice to have what basketball, baseball, and football players have—a contract. A golfer is always a free agent."

Kristy wound up developing a hiatal hernia in those early years. "It was purely stress. I got advice to watch what I was eating and do all that, but I knew it was stress."

D. A. tried to understand. He says now, "I was always taught by my dad to get my emotions out and express them. Kristy held them in. I didn't always know how stressed she really was. I think by holding those in, worrying about things in the early years, that probably was the cause of the hernia. But she didn't show that externally."

After her hernia developed, Kristy told herself to just stop worrying. "I realized I could not live and die with every golf shot," she says. "I could not be checking the money list all the time." Instead, when D. A. was playing, Kristy would team up with another player's spouse and chat as they walked around the golf course. She always knew how D. A. was playing and what his score was, but she didn't let herself get all tied up in knots about every detail of the round. "You can't do that and keep your sanity."

"I was a good player," D. A. says, "but I wasn't the guy who was destined to be on the PGA Tour. I had to earn my way and keep improving. Her stress was, 'Okay, we got there. Can we stay there?' Because you have to keep earning your money each year. Later in life, for her, it was that she wanted me to be able to achieve my accomplishments rather than making money for us to survive."

Kristy agrees. "Later, I think that was my biggest thing. I wanted him to feel fulfilled and be happy. I knew we were going to be taken care of no matter what. If something happened to him, if he were injured and couldn't play golf—I knew he was smart enough. He would find something else, and he always has. But as his wife, you want him to be successful. I know how hard he's worked all of his life. I wanted that to come to fruition."

Also, Kristy did not want to live her life comparing it to someone else's. It was not in her nature. "You want to be able to root for everybody. I would never pull against anyone because it is not a good way to live," she says.

It helped that D. A. himself always had a positive attitude. "Very rarely did he not have a good perspective on things," she says. "He might have been disappointed, and he might talk to me about it later, but he was always able to turn around and find the positive. That made it easier for me that he wasn't moaning and groaning. He just had a really good attitude about it."

She would say to family or friends who would bemoan how something turned out, "Nobody has the right to be more upset than D. A. He is the one who is out there hitting each shot." She felt it was her responsibility to be there for him. "My job was to be his cheerleader."

Fortunately, Kristy and D. A. had strong Midwestern values that kept them from feeling the pressure to live too high whenever a windfall of winnings would appear. Instead, they always had an eye to living within their means and retaining that sense of being grounded. "You try to put some of the winnings away when you have good years, so you protect yourself," Kristy says. "We were raised in the Midwest. We've had a good life. But we've also been wise about how we spend our money. We wanted to be able to send our kids to college and do all those things."

When Katey was about three, D. A. had a wrist injury that required surgery and significant down time from playing. This made him start thinking that he needed to have more going on than playing golf. He wound up partnering with some colleagues to launch his golf course design company, now known as Weibring Wolford Golf Design, with projects around the world. Being entrepreneurial along with professional golf was how D. A. ensured that he would always be able to provide for the family's future. That business management degree he was earning when he met Kristy has not gone to waste.

By the time D. A. started on the Champions Tour, times had certainly changed. Kristy didn't have to wonder how things were going when she couldn't be at a tournament; she could check online to find out what was happening on the course. Sometimes the telecasts were not live, but she would already know the outcome from the computer. A couple of times, she already knew that D. A. won. This would take away the stress of watching, because sometimes the telecasters are overly dramatic. "On the Champions Tour with D. A. playing," she says, "it wasn't anywhere near as stressful as the regular tour. I knew no matter what, we were going to be fine."

Kristy always enjoyed going with D. A. on the Champions Tour because it was as if you were traveling with your family. There was so much history with everyone else there—the players on the tour had been playing golf together for so long. "When you hit your fifties and sixties, you realize what is important in life," Kristy says. "Everyone's kids are either getting married or having your grandchildren. We are all experiencing having older parents or our parents passing away." They could share their experiences and help one another by being good friends who listen.

In the Champions Tour, D. A. won five times. Kristy didn't get to see the first four, but she was there for the fifth win—the Senior Players Championship. "That was pretty exciting," she says. "D. A. has been retired for almost four years now. He had a back injury that doesn't bother him unless he goes to play golf. Mostly, he does not play." He misses it but is overall happy with where he is in life. "It isn't easy. But he's doing okay now." Kristy smiles. "In fact, he just took our oldest grandson, who is seven, to play nine holes. That's the first time he's played nine holes in a while. They had a great time."

Now relocated from Plano to Frisco, Texas, Kristy and D. A. have set up the Weibring Family Foundation, which supports many organizations, including schools, athletics, cancer research, and one that is very special to their family: the Dancers Give Back Dallas charity. Originally started in 2007 in Buffalo, New York, Dancers Give Back has groups in several branch cities, including Dallas, that are united in their fight to support young-adult cancer patients and their families. It was a perfect choice for Kristy in several ways. Daughters Katey and Allie, of course, grew up dancing. Katey dances professionally, as does her husband, Cory. Allie, too, had her bout with Hodgkin's lymphoma, so the cause is close to their hearts. The first annual DGB-Dallas charity event took place in January 2014, and the entire family participated. In two days, they had raised $28,000. All of the proceeds went toward pediatric, adolescent, and young adult cancer research and patient support. This organization wants families to unite, give back, and dance toward finding a cure.

Kristy remains down to earth in every regard. "I feel like my life is really not that exciting, to be honest," she says with a laugh. "D. A. and I feel like we've had a great life, with playing on the tour and all the people that we've been able to meet. We're just so blessed."

14 Being a Golfer's Wife

The last thing I ever expected when I was a young woman was to fall in love with a blind date who happened to be a passionate golfer. Acceptance and compromises along the way on both sides have made for a happy marriage.

Raising two daughters was a team effort. Steve would sit down with Laura and go over her homework assignments, while I would cook dinner and entertain Emily. We were very much hands-on parents, but we let them make choices and mistakes.

Golf is one of Steve's jobs since he retired, along with the chief dishwasher position. Unfortunately, neither are paid positions. That's okay, because with golf he has worked hard to afford the luxury, and it brings him pleasure most of the time. He loves the competition, and when he wins, I am thrilled for him. With dishwashing, he is rewarded with food on the table—some gourmet meals and others very basic. He devours them all.

I made a conscious decision not to be a golf widow. I had to be willing to learn a new sport. It did require more work than I ever anticipated. Who knew hitting that little white ball with accuracy could be so challenging? I certainly did not, because my husband made it look effortless. Steve's patience with me in teaching was another activity that we could bond over. It became part of a dating ritual. In the beginning, he would let me bend a few rules, like kicking a ball out of the rough. Now he challenges me and encourages me to hit some of those difficult shots. I'm always thankful when I hit out of those treacherous trees and the ball doesn't strike one and come flying back at me.

The male-bonding aspect of his buddy golf trips works for us. It provides a little break for both of us. I can enjoy solitude, do something with friends, or visit family. When he arrives home content and exhausted, the shared stories are hilarious and sometimes unbelievable.

My mental and physical therapy regimen includes working out by walking the beach, swimming, biking, rollerblading, and simply enjoying the beautiful outdoors. Golf enters into this mix about once a week, depending upon the weather. Steve will join in my outdoor activities occasionally and more frequently when we have out-of-town guests. Our daughters, their husbands, and my darling grandchildren all love coming to the beach. It's wonderful having a home in Florida to share with family and guests where entertaining is just a few steps out the door.

It is my hope that Steve will be able to play golf well into his eighties. If so, I'll always be right by his side and still be trying to beat him on a golf hole straight up! Fore!

LIST OF CHARITIES

The Brandt & Mandy Snedeker Foundation
The mission of the Snedeker Foundation is to help underprivileged children across the country, but particularly in the middle Tennessee area, with an emphasis on encouraging success in the classroom and in their respective sports.

Brighter Days Foundation, brighterdaysfoundation.com
Jason and Ellie Day's Brighter Days Foundation is working to meet basic needs, give hope, and support child-serving organizations in central Ohio.

Charley Hoffman Foundation, charleyhoffmanfoundation.org
Established in 2009 by Charley and Stacy, this foundation raises funds for charities benefiting children in their native and adopted hometowns of San Diego and Las Vegas.

Crystal Coast Hospice House, crystalcoasthospicehouse.org
Crystal Coast Hospice House provides exceptional care in a homelike setting for the terminally ill who live in their service region in North Carolina.

Micaela's Army Foundation, micaelasarmyfoundation.org
The foundation's mission is to raise and donate money to help fund cancer research, education, awareness, and patient support for the cancers that affect children, adolescents, young adults, and their families.

Jacobsen Youth Initiative,
oga.org/junior-golf/jacobsen-youth-initiative
Founded by the Jacobsen Family, the Jacobsen Youth Initiative supports and encourages young people to play the game of golf. It promotes etiquette and teaches lifetime skills.

Juvenile Diabetes Research, jdrf.org
JDRF leads the fight against type 1 diabetes (T1D) by funding research, advocating for policies that accelerate access to new therapies, and providing a support network for millions of people around the world impacted by T1D.

ACKNOWLEDGMENTS

I'd like to acknowledge the following people:

Sue Rhea is a dear friend, who had faith in me and set me up with my first interview. From there, my list grew, and I'm so appreciative!

The Golfers' Wives:

Ellie Day

Stacy Hoffman

Jan Jacobsen

Lisa Lye

Mandy Snedeker

Sarah Strange

Kristy Weibring

Thank you for your faith, trust, and candid interviews. Your patience in getting this book published is so appreciated. It has been a long journey, and I am grateful for your support.

Laura Matthews, my editor extraordinaire. She is not a golfer but took on this project to bring a new perspective. Through her eyes, even the nongolfer will understand this book.

Thanks also to the team at Amplify Publishing: Naren Aryal, Matthew Gonsalves, Claire Pask, Nina Spahn, and Julia Steffy.

Above all, Lord, thank you for your guidance and strength along this literary journey, and in life! I pray this book will raise significant funds for all the charities it supports.

ABOUT THE AUTHOR

For some, golf comes naturally, but for others, they marry into it! Unbeknownst to Janet as she was walking down the aisle, her husband-to-be was a die-hard golfer. Not necessarily wanting to be the quintessential "golf widow" after the honeymoon, Janet headed for the fairway. (Although, for her, it was more like the rough.)

Janet Thompson lives with her husband, Steve, in Florida and New Hampshire. The pair enjoys golfing, hiking, biking, and spending time with their five young grandchildren. In the summers, Janet volunteers her time for the Gundalow Company, sailing with school-age children and adults on the Piscataqua River in a replica of a boat launched in 1886.

Janet believes, "When taking up golf, a sense of humor and the ability to bend a few rules helps!" Had she read a book like this before she started playing the game, it would have made a difference in her love/hate relationship with golf.